Advance Praise for
Beyond the Sea

"This is a book everyone should read. A true behind-the-scenes story about leadership, humility, and duty in the navy and in life. Robert 'Navy Bob' Roncska is a real-life American hero and role model."

Daniel Silva
New York Times Bestselling Author

"An inspiring foundation for radical success within complex high-stakes organizations, *Beyond the Sea* speaks directly from a fascinating life of hard-won experience. With genuine humility, Bob Roncska writes from the heart, drawing on success and failure alike. We join him across a unique and fascinating sweep of decades as he personally discovers, implements, and unleashes the power of leading with love. Bob is the single most caring and invested leader with whom I have ever served. He has so much to teach us all about how to build the very best winning cultures."

Rear Admiral Jim Waters, USN
(provided in my personal capacity and not
an endorsement by the DoD or the US Navy)

"From the first time I met 'Navy Bob,' it was evident he was a special breed of leader living out of his heart. In *Beyond the Sea*, he has moved well beyond the typical lists of leadership traits and how-tos to invoke the most powerful force in humanity—love. Reminding us of the essential needs of the people we lead and enriching his guidance with compelling and relatable real-life stories, Bob shows the power of love in building a rich culture, getting results, and changing lives. He shows that love shapes our own motivations and awakens the commitment of others. It is what we need in our leaders today."

Steven C. Preston
President and CEO, Goodwill Industries International

"Our country is blessed by patriots and people of integrity like 'Navy Bob' Roncska. Molded by examples of leadership, sacrifice, and love throughout his personal life and career, Bob Roncska is a man of character and compassion and the epitome of a servant leader. His heartfelt and beautifully written book reminds us that a good life is about service and caring for the well-being of others. I am delighted he has shared his lessons learned about different styles of leadership. His experiences will surely encourage readers to approach personal and professional decisions the way he did—with humility and courage and love."

Anita McBride
Former Chief of Staff to Mrs. Laura Bush, Executive in Residence, School of Public Affairs, American University

"I remember well President George W. Bush and First Lady Laura Bush teaching us that government can help a person out, but it can never heal a person's heart. They led with love and principles, and our favorite Navy Bob has captured their approach well in his must-read book on the best way to lead."

Dana Perino
Former White House Press Secretary for President George W. Bush

"Bob gave the American people the gift of an exemplary career of public service, and now with this book, he gives us the gift of some extraordinary lessons on leadership, decision-making, and compassion. *Beyond the Sea* is a warm, engaging, and fun journey through Bob's life, where he distills what he experienced and learned in ways that leave the reader with a how-to manual on becoming a successful leader."

Faryar Shirzad
Tech Executive and Former Deputy National Security Advisor for International Economics

"'Navy Bob' Roncska has the rare and powerful combination of leadership in the crucible of naval operations and business. There's nothing more intense and critical than commanding a nuclear sub to understand what true leadership requires. He has flawlessly captured these lessons, perfectly offering his experiences for application by leaders in any industry."

Alden Philbrick
Chairman, CEO and President, Oxford Finance

"As military aide to President Bush, Navy Bob carried immense responsibility, serving with humility and compassion. It was a privilege to work alongside Bob, and it's an honor to recommend his book—it sets the tone for the kind of leaders we need most."

Jared Weinstein
Former Special Assistant to President George W. Bush
and Founding Partner, Thrive Capital

"When I think of Navy Bob, one word immediately comes to mind: trust. This is a man who was entrusted with the entire fate of the free world at his fingertips. As you read *Beyond the Sea*, you'll learn that the secret to earning unqualified trust—from the president on down—is leading through love and compassion. His story is as gripping as it is inspiring. Bob burned the boats for his country. This is a must-read!"

Matthew Higgins
Author, *Burn the Boats*

"An inspiring tale of purpose, principles, and excellence, *Beyond the Sea* will help readers live a good life full of meaning and impetus. Navy Bob's sea stories are entertaining, informative, and prophetic. Your professional and personal journey will reap benefits from experiencing his courageous impatience and uncommon insight into the dimensions and applications of leadership."

Jeffrey Kuhlman, MD, MPH
White House Physician 2000 – 2013, Physician to the Forty-Fourth
President and Chief Quality and Safety Officer, AdventHealth

"I was honored to serve alongside Navy Bob during his time as the presidential military aide for the forty-third president. I came to know him as a remarkably dedicated leader during our many travels together. I found his personal story both insightful and compelling. I wholeheartedly endorse his focus on the central roles love and trust play in leadership and feel his refreshing perspectives make his book a must-read!"

John I. Pray, Jr., Brigadier General, USAF (Ret.)
President and CEO, Operation Homefront

"Dr. Bob Roncska's book, *Beyond the Sea: Leading with Love*, is an enthralling study of practical leadership. I have read countless leadership books, most of which are formulaic, mechanistic, or simply experiential. This is a significant paradigm shift, rightly premised on the importance of 'love first.' If your heart is right, inspirational leadership and organizational success will follow. Although Navy Bob credits many leaders for their influence on his leadership style, I believe the attributes he highlights in this book have been a deep-rooted part of his DNA his entire life. This book is a must-read for those who are serious about improving their leadership skills."

Bruce Grooms, VADM (Ret.), USN

"This book is captivating from beginning to end. Bob's personal story, his leadership, and the lessons he shares chart a course for anyone tasked with leading others. We all face challenges, and Bob's message reminds us to stay the course by leading with love—cultivating compassion, building trust, and ensuring every member of the team understands their purpose."

Chris Webb, Captain
U.S. Merchant Marines

"This book is a masterful tapestry of life-changing lessons from a multi-faceted career with the consistent result of success. Jesus's command to love your neighbor as yourself is not a suggestion. Navy Bob gets it. He is a compassionate and enlightened leader who motivates with love. His book is a must-read."

David Sona, Captain (Ret.), USN

"*Beyond the Sea* is outstanding—a must-read for anyone in a leadership role. Captain 'Navy Bob' Roncska illustrates love is foundational for successful leadership. His experiences can be utilized at the highest levels from championship athletic teams to Fortune 500 companies to healthcare organizations. This book is applicable for everyone seeking to strengthen their personal relationships and build high-functioning teams during chaotic and rapidly changing times."

Kevin D. Accola, MD
Executive Director, Cardiothoracic Surgery, AdventHealth

"In his new book, *Beyond the Sea*, Captain 'Navy Bob' Roncska offers a riveting account of leadership built on trust and psychological safety to create highly reliable teams capable of transformational change. This book is a must-read for new and seasoned healthcare leaders alike."

Eric M. Deshaies, MD, MBA, FAANS, FAC
Neurosurgeon and Chief Physician Executive,
AdventHealth Medical Group

"Dr. Navy Bob, my favorite heaven-sent apostle of leader-member exchange (LMX) leadership theory, paints a boldly colored story of his adventures as a hero with the heart of a *Top Gun* Maverick toward loyal companions who are loved much like Goose. Bob's adventures illustrate our theory of following the second law of innovative leadership by collaboration."

Dr. George Bernard Graen
Chief Scientist, LMX project

BEYOND THE SEA

LEADING WITH LOVE FROM THE **NUCLEAR NAVY** TO THE **WHITE HOUSE** AND **HEALTHCARE**

Robert "Navy Bob" Roncska

ROBERT "NAVY BOB" RONCSKA, DBA

Ballast Books, LLC
www.ballastbooks.com

Copyright © 2024 by Robert Roncska

No part of this book may be reproduced in any form or by any electronic or mechanical means including information storage and retrieval systems, without permission in writing from the author. The only exception is by a reviewer, who may quote short excerpts in a review.

The author has tried to recreate events, locales, and conversations from his memories of them. To maintain their anonymity in some instances, the author has changed the names of individuals and places.

The views expressed in this publication are those of the author and do not necessarily reflect the official policy or position of the Department of Defense or the U.S. government. The public release clearance of this publication by the Department of Defense does not imply Department of Defense endorsement or factual accuracy of the material.

ISBN: 978-1-955026-20-8

Printed in Hong Kong

Published by Ballast Books
www.ballastbooks.com

For more information, bulk orders, appearances, or speaking requests, please email: info@ballastbooks.com

To my wife, Stephanie;
my father, Raymond Roncska;
Vice Admiral Bruce E. Grooms;
and the great men and women I served with
throughout my career.

Contents

Author's Note   i
Don't Mess with *Texas*   iii

PART ONE: FORMATIVE YEARS   1
1 — A Foundation of Love   3
2 — The Power of Words   7
3 — Part of a Team   13
4 — Love and Standards   23
5 — The Problem with Fear   31

PART TWO: INVALUABLE LESSONS OF LEADERSHIP STYLES   41
6 — Awakening   43
7 — The Erosion of Trust   57
8 — The Strength of a Brotherhood   67
9 — Finding a Purpose   73

PART THREE: LEADING WITH LOVE AT THE HIGHEST LEVELS   81
10 — A Sense of Belonging   83

11 — The Need for Compassion   93
12 — Built on Trust   99

PART FOUR: APPLYING LEADERSHIP LESSONS   109
13 — The Effects of Apathy   111
14 — Time for an Intervention   117
15 — Where the Magic Happens   131
16 — Building Leaders   143
17 — Fairwinds and Following Seas   151

PART FIVE: LEADERSHIP BEYOND THE SEA   163
18 — Beyond the Sea   165
19 — Making a Difference   169
20 — Building Relationships   179
21 — Final Thoughts   189

Epilogue   195
Acknowledgments   197
Appendix   201
Endnotes   203

AUTHOR'S NOTE

"We can't help everyone, but everyone can help someone."

—Ronald Reagan

As I reflect on more than half a century of life, I am so thankful for the many individuals who helped shape and mold me. My character and mindset directly result from the people and events that left indelible marks on my psyche. I am a product of good and bad experiences, but the kindness of others has woven the tapestry of my life and served as my fuel. I feel driven to emulate the goodness I have experienced and multiply it exponentially for others.

While writing this book, I had a minor stroke that served as a wake-up call. Fortunately, I have recovered completely. However, it reminded me that life is precious and precarious, and I want to spend my remaining days serving others and leaving a legacy of love and encouragement. In this book, which is part memoir, part leadership blueprint, I wish to share my journey in hopes that you, too, will be inspired to seek ways to uplift and serve others, making each day memorable and meaningful for those in your circle of influence.

Throughout, you will read many of my favorite quotes, which reflect my passion and support the message I wish to convey. I hope that within these stories of my life, you will see the beauty of the people who have taught me about love and leaving a legacy. I want to honor these heroes of mine by demonstrating how they have influenced my thoughts, words, and actions. In this work, my children and other readers will come to know and feel the impact of the prominent people who have shown me what it means to love unconditionally and sacrificially. May it serve as an inspiration—after all, helping others is the core of living a good life.

Don't Mess
with
Texas

"Of all the branches of men in the forces there is none which shows more devotion and faces grimmer perils than the submariners."

—Winston Churchill

"This isn't good," I whispered to my executive officer as a sub-hunting aircraft flew directly overhead, taking up the full view of our 377-foot fast-attack nuclear submarine's periscope.

I swallowed hard and felt my pulse quicken, but I knew I needed to project a calm and steady presence. I managed to order "DOWN SCOPE!" in a swift, loud voice.

As we waited, listening with our highly sensitive sonar for additional flyovers, I looked around the silent room at the thirty sets of eyes trained on me. I could feel my crew's fear and apprehension as they awaited my direction.

Some of the faces that stared back were old and weathered, but many were the fresh faces of young men who had joined the navy straight out of high school. They hailed from states across the nation, including our ship's namesake, Texas. My sailors were the best our country had to offer. I thought about their fathers and mothers who had entrusted me with their care.

Our two-billion-dollar, Virginia-class submarine was on a classified mission in unfriendly waters thousands of miles from her home port of

Pearl Harbor, Hawaii. Our task was to gather information about the area, collect special signals of interest, and observe our adversary conduct a certain secret event. The mission required gliding unseen beneath the surface in close proximity to numerous formidable combatants. It was a tall but achievable order for a ship with the motto "Don't mess with *Texas!*"

During the operation, we had deviated from the standard protocol of a continuous 360-degree periscope sweep, opting instead to direct the periscope's limited restricted field of vision toward our adversary's activities in anticipation of the imminent event. I had based this decision on the examples set by previous commanding officers during similar high-stakes missions, and I considered the departure from normal procedure an acceptable risk.

But when I detected a subtle, audible shift in the radar noises emanating from the speaker in the control room, I ordered my officer of the deck to do a 360-rotational view with the periscope, then focused on the dozens of electronic boards surrounding me. That was when the enemy aircraft filled our screen.

If we were spotted, our adversary would likely box us in and force an emergency surface, spelling the end of our critical mission and causing public scrutiny and embarrassment of our fleet and, more broadly, our government. Counter-detection could even jeopardize the safety of our ship and, worst of all, my crew.

As we waited below the murky waters, listening for sounds of the plane's return, my mind raced and my pulse boomed in my ears. Timing was critical to our mission. In fact, I wondered if we'd already missed the event we were there to observe. With our periscope down, it was impossible to know.

It felt like an eternity, but after a few minutes ticked by with no indication that the aircraft had circled back, I ordered the scope to be raised again.

Tension filled the air as my operations officer studied his surveillance equipment in the adjacent room. His deep voice suddenly broke the silence as he broadcast a pre-rehearsed counter-detection alert: "Control, this is the operations officer. FIRECRACKER! FIRECRACKER! FIRECRACKER!"

It was what I had been dreading. I knew that to avoid catastrophe, it was time to take evasive measures, though I was reluctant to fail at our critical mission with its large price tag. For a moment, I considered that my operations officer might be wrong and that our adversary had detected something other than our ship. But the chances of such a coincidence seemed near zero.

My gut told me they had us and we needed to act. I knew exactly what to say. I had played this scenario out in my head many times and rehearsed the order: "Make your depth four hundred feet. All ahead standard. Left full rudder. This is the captain. I have the conn."

But before I articulated the words, my XO, Gary Montalvo, anticipated my intention and stopped me. Stepping in front of me, he held up his hand and said in a voice loud enough for all to hear, "Captain, Captain, wait! We're already screwed; let's see if we are pregnant."

Gary knew that my decision to deviate from standard procedure made me anxious to ensure the safety of the crew. While he thought there was a good chance that we had been counter-detected, he also saw what the guilt of my recent decision caused me to miss—the extended time it took for the aircraft to circle back was odd and gave us reason to hope that we had *not* been seen. We might not be "pregnant" after all.

Gary didn't want to flinch without just cause. He knew the decision I was about to make would be irreversible and mean mission failure. My actions would be critiqued by high-ranking officials, and if subsequent analysis showed that we had not been counter-detected, my decision would be used as a textbook example of what not to do on a mission.

In order to protect me, Gary put his own credibility on the line and openly challenged my authority. Since we had a long-established relationship of trust and respect, there was no part of me that doubted he spoke out of love, loyalty, and concern for me and the crew. So, I listened while Gary explained his thoughts.

Still, I was uneasy with the idea of delaying, and the weight of the seemingly no-win situation pressed down upon me.

Then, another sailor spoke up. "Maybe it wasn't us the aircraft detected. Something doesn't make sense."

Several others began to chime in.

As they spoke, I became convinced; my original assessment of the situation didn't feel right. I finally agreed: "Let's see if we are pregnant."

We stayed put—which was far more stressful than running. We felt conspicuous and vulnerable in our steel capsule, all the time expecting our adversary to react. But they continued their operation as if unaware of our presence. It seemed my XO had been right.

At the conclusion of the event, we returned to our home port, riding high on the accomplishment of a successfully completed mission vital to national security.

But what had given Gary the courage to risk speaking up? In short, mutual trust and understanding. He knew that I would listen to what he had to say rather than punish him because I knew he would only speak out of the best of intentions. We had each other's backs. We shared a sense of purpose, foundational principles, and a relentless drive for excellence. Gary and the other members of my crew protected each other like family. We'd built a high-functioning culture that allowed us to achieve success even in great moments of crisis. Our culture was legendary.

In this book, I will provide tools you can implement with your own teams. Research shows that leadership *can* be taught.[1] If you use the basic principle of familial love as the core of your mission, you can build a legendary culture. I will offer many examples of how caring for my team members led to success and extraordinary results.

Of course, love alone isn't enough. I will also explain how trust, standards, purpose, and accountability all play a role. Individually, these foundational principles cannot yield success; they need each other to flourish. Building a culture with all of them is in itself an act of love.

Though I focus on stories of success, I believe it's important to reflect on times of failure and poor examples of leadership as well. I have come to realize my failures happened when I lost sight of the necessary foundation of love. In those moments, I focused on the mission, myself, or avoiding unpleasant consequences. The Bible's well-known chapter on love says, "Love is patient and kind; love does not envy or boast; it is not arrogant or rude. It does not insist on its own way; it is not irritable or resentful; it does not rejoice at wrongdoing but rejoices with the truth."[2] I've found that when I act on what love *is*, instead of what love is *not*, my results are more significant.

I cannot emphasize enough that the story I've just shared with you would not have been possible without a culture rooted in love. If Gary hadn't believed I cared for him, he would have hung me out to dry and allowed me to make a decision he believed could be wrong. If the sailor who supported the XO hadn't felt safe speaking up and hadn't known his CO cared for him, he never would have risked the possible backlash.

Prior to me taking command, the USS *Texas* was the worst-performing ship in the squadron, but in just a year and a half, my team and I turned that record around, making the *Texas* the top ranked of the squadron's ten submarines. We also had the highest retention in the Pacific Fleet for two consecutive years and scored the best possible grade on a rigorous nuclear engineering exam. It wasn't due to my intelligence, tactical prowess, or charisma that USS *Texas* succeeded; instead, it was my ability to nurture strong connections based on familial love. I'll give concrete examples of how we accomplished this transformation. I'll also share how leaders from the Navy SEALs to the White House inspired their teams with unconditional love. Lastly, I will show you how this formula helped me, as executive director of quality and safety for one of the largest healthcare systems in the US, to transform cultures in healthcare.

**THE FIRST JOB
OF LEADERSHIP
IS TO LOVE PEOPLE.**

—RICK WARREN—

PART ONE: FORMATIVE YEARS

—CHAPTER 1—

A FOUNDATION OF LOVE

"The most powerful leadership tool you have is your own personal example."

—JOHN WOODEN

Love is universally experienced. Countless songs celebrate or pine for it, and every major world religion extols its virtues. If you ask my wife, an elementary educator, she'll tell you that it's what every child coming into a classroom needs and wants. As a leader, I believe it is what every team member needs on some level as well. Of course, I'm not talking about romantic love, but rather a familial love that can make work life better and more fulfilling. This kind of love has shaped both my life and my leadership style.

DEMONSTRATIONS OF LOVE

I learned my first lessons on love during my childhood.

Witty and outgoing, my mother was always the life of the party. Everyone enjoyed being around her. She cared for people and had an innate way of knowing what was needed, whether it was through celebrating events, dropping off groceries or casseroles, or simply helping in any way she could.

She particularly showed her love through food. From a Polish family big on eating, my mother piled our dinner table with more than was needed for one meal. Our diet was rich in meat and bread, and we were encouraged to finish every morsel. Doing so was a sign of our returned affection. Over time, we all physically showcased that affection in our waistlines.

This language of love found in the kitchen was a trait passed down from my grandmother, who would serve us piles of bacon with our breakfasts and often say to me, "Eat, Bobby, eat!" Generous love poured from both women through their unspoken language of food—not just to family but to all in their communities.

Once, as a teenager, I was tasked with delivering my mother her forgotten lunch. I stood outside the admissions building of the state university where she worked. It was a hot day, and I was annoyed to be waiting in the sun while Mom finished what she was doing. I loitered around the entrance, staring at the weeds that grew in the gaps of the cracked sidewalk and listening to cars passing by. A woman exiting the building noticed me and probably thought I looked menacing and out of place with my large frame and irritated expression.

"Can I help you?" she asked.

"No," I replied, "I'm just waiting for my mom, Eileen. She forgot her lunch." I held up the paper sack as proof. A smile spread across the woman's face as she realized who I was.

"Oh my gosh, you must be Bobby!" she began to gush. "Your mother is the nicest person in the world!"

The coworker carried on about all the helpful things my mom did for the students and the wonderful treats she would bake and bring into the office. She told me how organized and efficient my mom was and how the place couldn't run without her expertise.

By the time my mother ran out to grab her lunch and give me a hug, I was no longer annoyed about having to wait. Instead, I was filled with pride.

The impression my mom made on people inspired me. I wanted to attend closely and lovingly to my coworkers and others around me in the same way Eileen Roncska did.

In contrast to my mother, my father was the silent type. He chopped wood, bailed hay, and labored on the family farm most of his life. He also served as a mechanic at the local power plant. Through all of this work, he developed an incredible strength that wasn't immediately apparent because of his small stature.

We lived in a modest two-bedroom, one-bath home my dad had inherited. He was always proud of the money he saved by growing hay and vegetables, raising cows and chickens, and even chopping wood to heat our home. I have vivid memories of him showing off our low energy bills to friends and family.

Dad's love and desire to please us drove him to work extreme hours. One frigid evening after working a twelve-hour shift, he got home to find a heifer had broken through her enclosure and escaped. I remember watching his entire being droop as I heard his exasperated sigh. His eyes were heavy with exhaustion, but he somehow mustered the energy to retrieve the wayward cow. After hours of chasing the frightened heifer, he successfully brought her home and then collapsed into bed.

In the weeks leading up to Christmas, my dad worked extra shifts to pay for our presents. He thought that giving us amazing gifts demonstrated his love and proved that he was a good provider. He always wanted to ensure our wish lists were fulfilled and that we had our heart's desires, constantly putting us first. At times, I took advantage of his generosity and asked for things I knew were beyond our budget and his comfort level.

Once, I pushed my dad to buy me a motorcycle. He was extremely hesitant because his own life had been riddled with loss and tragedy, and the thought of putting me in danger made him cringe. Nonetheless, I knew he liked to give us whatever we asked for, so I kept at him. Eventually, he gave in and worked additional shifts to save money for a used dirt bike.

The 125cc dirt bike was by no means a powerful or excessively fast machine, but my dad still worried I would get hurt. He set boundaries and warned me to stay off nearby railroad ridges. But, like any twelve-year-old, I pushed the limits and went out of bounds. Inevitably, my bike and I separated one day, resulting in a minor incident that led to bloody forearms and mud from head to toe. When I approached my dad afterward, I could see the look of horror on his face. I didn't know then why he was so concerned, partly because I was young but mostly because I did not understand the traumatic events that had shaped him.

AGAPE LOVE

When he was only three, my father's life took an unexpected and devastating turn. His pregnant mother and her unborn child died during childbirth. This tragedy began a cascade in which my father lost everything precious to him. His older half-brother left to join the army. His half-sister was sent away to live with their grandparents. My grandfather, unable to care for his young son alone and run his farm, decided to place my father in an orphanage. The confusion and pain my father must have felt as he was sent away are unimaginable to me.

He rarely talked about his time at the orphanage, but I know those lonely formative years left a yearning in my father for a family of his own.

When he finally had that family, his gratitude and love for us were deep and immeasurable.

One summer day, my uncle and cousin dropped by our farm unexpectedly to see if I could go bowling. My dad needed to get the hay bailed and relied on me to help. But there was always work to be done and the thought of spending time in a bowling alley with air conditioning, a Coke, and a slice of pizza was appealing. I looked at my dad, then at my uncle, and then back at my dad again, torn between doing what was right and doing what was fun. In the end, I chose bowling.

As I looked out the back window of my uncle's car, I watched my dad slump a little and walk off into the field. My choice to leave was a relatively small decision, but it still makes me feel guilty, knowing that I disappointed the man who had given me so much. His sacrifices and my selfish act are imprinted on my heart. Today, because I learned from his selfless example, I am driven to sacrifice for others, and my own sacrifices allow me to honor him in a small way.

Looking back at the type of love my father exhibited for us, I am reminded of the word "agape." Often seen as a specifically religious type of love, it simply means "unconditional love." I apply agape to my father's kind of love, giving it the weight and reverence it deserves.

I undoubtedly owe my love for family to my father. I learned from him how to lead with love. He took pride in his work and taught my brother and me how to do the same. With his gentle and caring guidance, he had us work right beside him as we grew into adulthood.

— CHAPTER 2 —

The Power of Words

"Words—so innocent and powerless as they are, as standing in the dictionary, how potent for good and evil they become in the hands of one who knows how to combine them."

—Nathaniel Hawthorne

Children sometimes say, "Sticks and stones may break my bones, but words will never hurt me." Although the chant is meant to show indifference to cruel words, most of us know the truth: words matter, and they *can* hurt. Like many others, I know the pain and joy that can come from someone else's words. Our hearts prompt our tongues to reveal our innermost thoughts. Sometimes that's a very good thing, but sometimes it's cruel.

Proverbs 12:18 (NIV) tells us, "The words of the reckless pierce like swords, but the tongue of the wise brings healing." Like any other human, I'm affected by kind and harsh words. And, of course, there are stories behind the words that trigger me.

A SPECIAL KIND OF HELL

When I was in second grade, I started to round out more than many of my classmates. In childhood, it's normal to widen a little before you lengthen, so to speak. I had a healthy appetite, and my body wasn't growing in height as fast as it was storing up reserves. The result, unfortunately, was a round face, with a round belly to match—and the beginning of several years of torment.

Locker rooms in the 1970s were a special kind of hell. My elementary school locker room had several stainless-steel poles with four or five shower heads each that shot out either scalding or frigid water in every direction. You could adjust the pressure to rip your skin off or barely mist your body.

On a good day, the locker room smelled like soap or baby shampoo. Usually, it smelled like mildew and sweaty sneakers. To add to the misery, we were expected to strip down and clean as a herd. I'm sure everyone felt self-conscious, even if they didn't show it. My bulging belly and chubby limbs amplified my embarrassment and made me a target.

A particular classmate, whom I will call Scott, decided it was his personal duty to comment on my physical traits. As most bullies do, Scott found joy in my pain. He taunted me constantly, from second grade through middle school. He especially loved to point out my large chest, which was developing less like a bodybuilder's and more like a girl's.

One day, running late from class, a few of us had to stand on the edges and wait for an available shower. Scott took full advantage of the situation and directed everyone's attention toward me. Because my belly obscured the view of my groin, Scott gleefully shouted, "Look, Bob doesn't have a dick!"

I turned bright pink with humiliation and fought to keep tears of embarrassment from running down my face. His horrible laugh echoed in my head.

I tried desperately to avoid him, but that really wasn't possible because I went to school in a small town. I dreaded gym class and carried anxiety home with me every day.

As the years passed, Scott amped up his verbal assaults, and they grew physical. He acted lewd and disgusting, and the locker room and showers became his hunting grounds. He peed in the locker room shower regularly to get a laugh or reaction from his crew. My breaking point came the day he turned and aimed right at me. I was thoroughly disgusted, and from then on, I refused to shower after PE.

His bullying didn't stop until I got serious about football. The physical demands of the sport coincided with my eventual growth spurt. I was still a big guy, but I had the type of physique that was advantageous on the football field and gave pause to bullies such as Scott. He didn't have much to say after I developed a more muscular build.

FOOTBALL LESSONS

Football brought with it many positives—not just the shedding of excess weight and Scott's comments but also the benefits of a caring coach and teammates.

My mother, however, wasn't keen on me playing football. More than anything, she was afraid I would get injured. In an effort to dissuade me, she kept throwing barriers in my way.

In the winter of my freshman year, my size and strength caught the eye of the varsity football coach. "Why aren't you playing football?" Coach Elvin asked me.

I was shocked. Frankly, it didn't seem like a possibility to me. Our football team was elite. They'd just missed going to the state championship by one touchdown the year before. I couldn't imagine they would be interested in me. I just shrugged.

"You could really contribute to our team," he insisted. "I want you to try out this summer."

That little interaction—the invitation to try out—was all I needed to get motivated.

Tryouts for the junior varsity team meant two practices a day. Two-a-days are common in football. Players were expected to be on the field in the morning and again in the late afternoon. I wanted to play so badly, this intense practice schedule didn't daunt me, but my mom was clear: no football. Still, I relentlessly cajoled.

Mom thought she had me when she agreed I could play but stipulated I had to find my own way to get to practice. Neither of my parents could possibly drive me with their work schedules. We lived five miles from town, and no other players lived in my vicinity. But Mom underestimated the work ethic she and Dad had instilled in me. I agreed to her terms, hopped on my bike, and set out to play ball.

Early mornings, large Ralston Purina trucks would rumble past me, threatening to blow over my Schwinn ten-speed as I made my way up the Urban Road hill. As I pedaled in the dark, I felt a twinge of fear, both for my safety and over doubts about my ability to perform on the field after the five-mile trek. But I was determined and did it. There and back. Every morning and afternoon.

I reaped a lot of benefits from cycling. The twenty miles of pedaling, combined with farm chores and football workouts, transformed me into a mass of muscle. I became known as "the tank." My strength, coupled with my will, became my signature trait. I didn't have a lot of finesse, but I could stop a guy in his tracks and move the ball forward if anyone got in my way.

That summer, Coach Gibbons replaced Coach Elvin. During tryouts, Coach Gibbons called me up to play on the varsity team, even though I was an inexperienced sophomore. I was elated. I'll never forget how good it felt to be wanted and appreciated.

Coach Gibbons said little, but when he spoke, his words had meaning. He believed in me; his affirmation fueled my drive to perform for him. Once, when being interviewed by the local paper, Coach Gibbons referred to me as "the team's workhorse." I made sure to live up to that description.

Our coach was by no means a soft man. He was actually a little rough around the edges, but he knew how to speak words of encouragement laced with inspirational calls to action, including two catchphrases that continue to influence me.

The first phrase he used nearly every day: "You either get better or get worse, but you don't stay the same." This sentiment pushed our team through grueling workouts and inspired us during games. The words were seared into our brains. I can still hear his booming voice as he barked out this challenge. And it's true, each day I will get better or worse. Nothing stays the same.

Coach Gibbons tried to do more than build football players. He dedicated his life to molding high school students into the next generation of leaders and good citizens. He cared about character as much as our skills. He understood that how we spent our time and with whom we spent it turned us into the men we would become. He would often bellow his second catch phrase: "If you lie down with dirty dogs, you will wake up with fleas."

Anytime Coach caught wind of one of his players engaging in questionable behavior or hanging around somewhere they shouldn't, he'd find a way to inject his dirty dog sentiment into our huddles. He watched out for us and would redirect us when needed. His comments reminded the team that he was watching over us and cared about our choices. He truly wanted us to succeed on and off the field.

One major asset of Coach's leadership was his ability to build team culture. He encouraged all of us to have each other's back. He helped us see that we all get better when one of us gets better. Older players took this to heart and spontaneously coached and encouraged younger players.

Although I was a tank, my feet were full of lead, and I was young and inexperienced. My teammate Lance pulled me aside one day and showed me how to juke (trick the opposing team's players with a feint). It was a foreign concept to me, not because I hadn't seen great running backs spin and weave to avoid defensive players on TV. I just hadn't made the mental connection that I needed to do the same. Instead, I was relying on sheer strength. Lance taught me the finesse needed to gain extra yardage. He was thoughtful as he pointed out my flaws, showed me some moves, and ribbed me when I seemed stuck in concrete.

It is the love language of some male adolescents to talk trash with their teammates. That type of teasing got in my head and helped me get better. My inclination was to run directly at an opponent in an effort to plow them over, which wasn't always the most prudent action. Lance would say things such as, "Why are you going straight at him, you stupid ass? Go right!"

His words actually fueled my learning and development until I could easily spin around oncoming defensive backs. Thanks to him, I gained yardage and increased my value to the team.

THE POWER TO BUILD OR BREAK

Words can build you up or break you down, depending on how they are intended. My coach and teammates used them to improve my performance and show their support; my locker room bully, of course, did none of that. My journey through adolescence created a powerful connection to the words of others.

Although my childhood was filled with great love at home, an underlying darkness began to creep in. As I got older, I became aware of conflict between my mother and father, an unhappiness that cast a shadow on both of them.

When I entered middle school, I began to notice my mother's underhanded comments toward my dad. Her words really bothered me, and I saw how deeply they cut into his soul. I know now she was holding on to childhood trauma and perhaps disappointment with how her life had turned out.

My maternal grandfather, who had been a prominent city councilman, could be frightening. When Mom was growing up, he frequently made disparaging comments about her appearance. She adored him anyway. It's too often the case that those you cherish are the ones who hurt you the most.

Mom's childhood home had been much bigger and her family more affluent than ours. Her youth was filled with material trappings. Public attention at political events had been a part of her father's existence, and I imagine Mom had reveled in the limelight along with him.

Unfortunately, these were things my dad could not give her. These were the things she'd hold over his head, often reminding him how he didn't meet her standards.

When Mom would say to Dad in a tone of disgust, "All you did was give me a two-room shack," I could see the heartbreak in his eyes.

It angered me when my mother said such things. I knew how hard my dad worked to give us everything we wanted. I saw the late nights, the extra shifts, and the exhaustion that resulted. I knew how much it meant to my dad that we had what he didn't have as a kid. He longed to prove to the world and his bride that he was worthy, and I watched as he expressed his love through actions and gifts. The two most important things to my dad were having a family and providing for us.

Mom got pregnant at the age of nineteen while she and Dad were dating. Her out-of-wedlock pregnancy initiated the typical response of the 1960s—a shotgun wedding. Mom often brought this up to remind Dad that she "*had* to marry him."

My dad adored my mom, and I knew she felt the same about him until those occasional dark moments when she didn't. About twice a year, they would have major arguments full of verbal abuse and rage. My mom would threaten divorce, and her words scarred the entire family. Dejected, my dad would flee to the local bar and drink himself into a stupor.

Mom stood two inches taller than my dad, and she knew he struggled with insecurity about his physical stature. When she was in a foul mood, she'd lash out at him to make him feel small, calling him names like "runt" or "little man." She seemed adept at breaking down his psyche.

The duality of her personality confounded me. As a teenager, I couldn't fathom how she could be kind and giving, even at home, but then abruptly turn and stab so deeply with her cruel words, leaving wounds that never healed. I now know she was in the beginning stages of mental illness.

I understand the power of harsh words because I faced my own tormentors, and because I witnessed the effects of my mom's insults on my father. Watching Dad's suffering hurt me to the core.

I also know the joy and encouragement that come from receiving acknowledgment and kind support. The times I have gotten positive recognition have made such a difference in my life. I became inspired to do the same for others and find ways to build up my family and teams.

When I was young, I determined that one day, I would be a provider and protector for everyone I loved. Like my dad, I feel driven to be a guardian and work hard. Perhaps even harder.

As I do this, I remind myself daily to choose my words wisely, because I know their power is lasting.

— CHAPTER 3 —

Part of a Team

"A team is not a group of people who work together. A team is a group of people who trust each other."

—Simon Sinek

In the 1980s, career aspirations for teenagers weren't a part of many conversations, and school counseling wasn't as robust as it is now. The meetings I had with my guidance counselor didn't provide much direction. After high school, most of us went to college in the State University of New York (SUNY) system, or we obtained local jobs. I didn't want to attend SUNY Fredonia like my brother did or get a job at one of the local plants.

I fell into college and my major somewhat haphazardly. I was clueless about the options outside my little world. Although I was pretty good at math and science, sitting around studying wasn't for me—I preferred a hands-on type of curriculum. Inspired by the movie *Top Gun* like so many other teenagers at the time, I thought I wanted to be a fighter pilot. My eyesight, however, wouldn't allow it.

WELCOME TO THE MILITARY

In my senior year, an alum of my high school told me about a college, Maine Maritime Academy, that focused on engineering, science, and transportation. The merchant marine serves as an auxiliary to the navy in times of war but is not part of the armed services—despite its military rigor. Maritime piqued my interest because its program included hands-on experience at sea. As part of the curriculum, students would spend time on a training ship, learning to become merchant mariners. It wasn't exactly flying jets, but ships seemed pretty cool too.

My mom had reservations about my ideas. She didn't like the thought of me going out of state. She just assumed I would attend school at SUNY Fredonia, like my brother. In her mind, it was the natural progression. Mom had difficulty telling me "no" when I set my mind to something, but she was also practical enough to recognize that in-state tuition was a better economic option for our family if college was in my future.

Knowing the ins and outs of the SUNY system, Mom looked for suitable alternatives to Maine Maritime. She found one at a merchant marine program in the Bronx. Nestled under the Throgs Neck Bridge, New York Maritime was a SUNY school option that would give me the practical experience I longed for.

With my mother's help, I set up a visit to the campus, began the application process, and chose a field of study. I had always liked math, especially when I could use it to solve a practical problem. Therefore, a degree in marine engineering seemed a natural fit. And just to make things more interesting, I added the nuclear option offered in the program. When I received my acceptance letter, I was beyond thrilled. I was set to begin my college experience in the summer of 1987.

That first week of school was a shock. Yes, I had been told it was regimented, and I had seen the uniforms on the students. I had also noticed the freshman—or "mugs" as they were called—running to class and rounding their corners (a funny sight when they stop at each corner suddenly and do a slow and precise ninety-degree turn). But I didn't quite make the connection that I had basically signed up for military service and training. The strict guidelines about what to bring should have been a clue, but somehow that didn't register with me—at least not until that first day of indoctrination.

The freshmen class was called out into the quad. We were a disheveled group, milling about aimlessly. There was some chatting and fooling around, a normal reaction to our first day of freedom away from our parents. That abruptly ended, however, when a line of indoctrination officers, members of the junior class, filed into the area. Their impressive dress and formation caught our attention. They moved as a unit, following the head indoctrination officer. He was their leader, and it showed.

That head officer barked orders to the line. They turned their flank to face us, and he pointed his sword in our direction. He bellowed in a clear and authoritative voice, "Class of 1991, let the indoctrination begin."

Around me, everyone was scrambling to move into line as he had commanded. I was quick on my feet and beat many of my classmates into formation. This reminded me a bit of football, and I didn't need to be told twice.

Before our line was complete, the juniors were in our faces yelling orders. Their derogatory comments were as quick as their commands. Anyone not capable was called out.

"Get down! Give me twenty! Stand straight! Shoulders back!" The instructions were demanding. As the new freshmen, we were expected to square the corners. We had to follow directions unflinchingly, without questioning authority. Welcome to the "military." Shape up or ship out.

The marching and drills lasted for two long weeks. It was nonstop conditioning. By the end of the indoctrination period, our rankings as freshmen were clear: we were at the bottom of the ladder.

INGENUITY AND INSPECTION

After the first day of chaos and harassment, I returned to my dorm, expecting to meet my roommate for the first time, but he and his belongings weren't in our room. I thought that was a little odd, and it added to my anxiety as I prepared my quarters for the first inspection. Already feeling homesick, my head was racing with all the future unknowns.

Would my roommate get in trouble for not being there? Would I be penalized if he didn't show up? That last thought was irrational, but after what I had experienced that day, I felt highly off kilter.

Finally, I heard a key slide into the lock and the doorknob turn. A short, young man with a big grin threw his backpack on the bed and said, "Hi, I'm James."

James showed up at Maritime woefully unprepared. He had brought very little with him—no sheets, no towels, and no footlocker. He only had clothes and toiletries. I soon discovered that he had thought he was entering a party school. James always wanted to take full advantage of every opportunity for a good time. This would become apparent a few nights later, but for now, we had to survive inspection.

It was scheduled two hours after his arrival. Room inspections caused problems for a lot of us. They were done routinely and at will. Everything had a place, and nothing should be out of order. Any demerits for infractions—such as not having the specified angle on a bedsheet's hospital corners—were applied to both roommates. It didn't matter who made the mess or who cleaned it up. We were equally in charge of the room and celebrated or suffered together. We were seen as a single entity.

It's difficult to pass an inspection of your bed when, like James, you don't have sheets. So, we scrambled to remedy the situation. Everyone had been given a standard-issue blanket for the top of their beds. We used this and one of my extra white towels to fold over the top, mimicking the required length of the sheet to be shown. We wrapped his pillow in another towel. Hospital corners were impossible, so we just prayed the indoctrination officer wouldn't look too closely.

We managed to polish the floors too. I sprayed the linoleum tile with furniture polish to give them a good shine. We didn't have a broom or mop, so James devised an outrageous plan. He told me to grab his legs and pull him across the floor. As we both laughed, I maneuvered him around our desks, chairs, and beds to pick up all the dust. It was hysterical *and* effective.

An indoctrination officer entered our room to do the white-glove inspection. James and I stood at attention before our beds and exchanged nervous glances. The officer looked at our floors. Impressed, he said, "Good job on the deck!"

Then, he inspected James's bed and noticed the towel. His eyes widened in disbelief. "What is that?"

"It's a towel, sir!" explained James with enthusiasm. "I forgot my sheets, sir! We had to improvise!"

I was certain we were sunk.

The indoctrination officer grinned and said, "Okay, carry on!"

I couldn't believe it! Our ingenuity must have impressed the inspector. At that moment, I knew James and I would be lifelong friends.

But despite my fondness for him, it wasn't all smooth sailing with James as a roommate. About a week into indoctrination, I was awoken at 1:00 a.m. to the sound of voices. I opened my eyes to see him leaning out of our second-story window. One by one, he pulled up three of his high school buddies and a case of beer into our room. His friends stood there with their shoulder-length hair and began to crack open the beers.

"Want one?" offered James.

I couldn't. I was too nervous. The longer James's friends stayed, the louder they got, and the more anxious I became. Fortunately, the night ended without incident. Soon after, I expressed my concerns over having late-night visitors, and he agreed that it wouldn't happen again.

A LOYAL TEAMMATE

Shortly after indoctrination, it was time to pick our permanent roommates. James and I had different majors, so we decided to find roommates with whom we shared more classes. I picked Chuck.

Although Chuck and I got along well, our cleanliness standards didn't align. I liked keeping my room in order; the lack of clutter helped me focus, and, of course, I didn't want to get demerits. I liked the freedoms awarded me from a good record. But Chuck's stuff was consistently scattered across the room, sabotaging our inspections. Room inspections weren't exactly at the top of Chuck's list of priorities. His motto was "2.0 and go," meaning he only aimed to get the C average he needed to graduate.

Always up for a good prank, I decided to teach Chuck a lesson. I enlisted the help of fellow freshman Jim Matola, who lived across the hall. Jim forged a letter from the regimental commander, Stan Okon, while I dictated the message, expressing the commander's great disappointment in Chuck's disregard for the importance of a tidy room. The "commander" told my roommate he expected the standards to be kept and sternly reprimanded him. Chuck was instructed to report immediately to the regimental commander's room to discuss this infraction.

Okon was a senior and the head student officer over the entire regiment. Everyone knew not to mess with him; we kept our distance to avoid his wrath. We wanted to escape extra training or work assignments that might include scraping a ship's hull, mopping the deck, or, most dreaded of all, scrubbing latrines.

Once written, the note was strategically placed on top of Chuck's bed. I sat at my desk with giddy anticipation. I had just seen Chuck about twenty minutes before, eating his lunch at the mess hall, and I expected him to return to the room before we went to our next class. The faked letter awaited him, and I could hardly focus on my studies as I imagined his reaction to what Jim and I had written. I planned to have a good laugh at his expense while I watched him panic.

The minutes ticked by, but Chuck didn't show. If I waited any longer, I would be late for class, so I rushed out to make it in time, leaving the letter on the bed. Chuck would be there, and I planned to guide him back to the room later that day to see the look on his face as he read the letter. But Chuck didn't come to class. I later learned he had ditched and gone back to the room after I left.

During class, I couldn't concentrate as I wondered why Chuck didn't show up. It was torture. I kept thinking about the letter. I debated internally, trying to decide if I should stay in class or get up and go. *Should I risk making the teacher mad by leaving early, or should I stay and potentially face the wrath of Stan? Will Chuck realize it's all a joke, or will he go to the commander? What will happen to him? What will happen to me?*

As I feared, Chuck had returned to the room and found the letter. He read the deceptive message and immediately reported to Okon. Even worse, the commander had been taking an afternoon nap, and Chuck's knock woke him up, adding to his irritation. Okon grabbed the paper, looked at the text, and snapped, "What the hell is this? I didn't write this letter!" Confused, Chuck apologized, dropped his head, and hightailed it to our room. Needless to say, he wasn't laughing when I got there.

Okon was determined to discover where the letter had come from and who to punish for it. Surprisingly, Chuck offered to go with me to speak to Okon and share the blame, hoping to avoid a class punishment. It didn't work. When we arrived in Okon's room, he wouldn't even let us talk.

Okon subjected me and the entire class to a brutal one-hour session of exercises at 5:00 a.m. The punishment itself was nothing compared to the guilt I felt for getting the rest of my classmates in trouble with my actions. But no one complained. No one said a word to rub in the extent of my screwup or make me feel worse. Rather, they banded together and took the group punishment as though it was justly earned by all. I was beginning to see what it meant to be on a team. I will never forget what it felt like to have Chuck and the rest of the class have my back at the expense of their own.

As it turned out, I became the regimental commander my senior year and had my own set of pranks and misdeeds to address. By then, I understood the wisdom of Okon's actions. He'd held me accountable and bonded me to my classmates with a punishment that was neither vindictive nor a mark on my permanent record. In fact, one-hour exercise sessions were a fairly routine part of our physical training.

As I meted out discipline my senior year and in the years that followed, I hoped to teach lessons of accountability and support for one's team, as Okon had taught me.

ONE HAND

There are two routes Maritime cadets can take through the program: deck or engine. "Deckies," working toward their third mate license, navigate the ship, deciding how and where the submarine goes. Engineers, working toward their third assistant engineer license, push the ship, ensuring the sub's propulsion system and other mechanisms are functioning properly.

Cadets spend two months training at sea each year. Participating as a sailor on an actual vessel builds technical skills and teaches the required standards of a merchant mariner. By the time students reach their senior year, they have spent the necessary six months underway, or at sea, for their certifications. This brings a wealth of opportunities for hands-on learning and a safe environment for trial and error as cadets man each station and learn the roles needed for full operations.

During the first weeks at Maritime, the freshmen were taught the importance of stepping in to help one another. "One hand" was a phrase we called out if we needed assistance or were in trouble. But often, "one hand" didn't even need to be said. Maritime students were a close-knit bunch, ready to jump in and offer aid without prompting.

Time at sea meant Atlantic crossings that took us to places like England, Italy, and Spain. While underway and at port, there were many opportunities to put the "one hand" concept into play. There are situations that can overwhelm a cadet, and almost all jobs require a second set of eyes to verify accuracy.

It's a beautiful thing when the team's strength shows itself in the silent reassurance of having one another's back, ensuring all is well and no person is left to suffer or fail. I'll admit that young mugs and cadets get themselves into situations that stretch the "one hand" practice. Nevertheless, shipmates come in full force when any need arises.

PARTYING LIKE A PIRATE

In the late 1980s and early '90s, Maritime students worked hard and played hard. I'm reminded of the expression "Work like a captain, party like a pirate." There is no doubt we lived by that mantra.

One Saturday, a group of friends made their way to Long Island for a house party. I rowed crew and couldn't drive over with them because we had a local regatta that day, but I planned to join them later that evening. Once the regatta was complete, I showered, changed, and made the long drive out with a fellow crew member. As we arrived at the party, we came upon the unexpected sight of a fistfight outside the home. About fifteen of my drunk buddies were fighting with eight local guys. It wasn't a fair fight. The unspoken rally of "one hand" led to a fifteen-on-eight melee that left the other guys angered at the imbalance of power. I jumped in to pull bodies apart and get the young men out before it escalated further. As they left, one of them yelled, "This isn't over!"

My buddies, hyped up on adrenaline and booze, couldn't help themselves. They recounted the skirmish with lots of "you should have seen that guy" and "they had it coming" talk. The congratulatory tone of their conversation didn't last long, however.

Soon after everyone calmed down and moved to the back patio, I saw the silhouettes of twenty men walking toward the yard. Their gait told me they were coming back to complete unfinished business. Instinctively, I yelled for my Maritime schoolmates to get back, and I told the owner of the house to go inside and call the police. Meanwhile, the mob stormed the patio, ready to even the score.

Fights broke out all over. As one of the only sober ones at the party, I knew the scene was dangerous. I moved from tussle to tussle, pulling people apart and screaming, "Get out!" But as soon as one fight stopped, another would break out. It was like playing a violent game of Whac-A-Mole. My efforts were futile, and my voice became hoarse from yelling at them to stop. I was exhausted, frustrated, and frankly pissed off that my friends' "beer muscles" were informing their decisions.

When I saw a figure run up to me, I thought at first that he was there to help me break up the fight. Instead, he placed the barrel of a handgun against my temple. I quickly realized how deadly the situation had become.

He started poking my head with the gun, screaming, "You think I'm screwing around? You think this is a joke?"

Since I was completely sober, it was fortunate that I was the one he chose to pull the gun on. I slowly put my hands up and backed away. "I'm trying to stop this. I am trying to help," I said.

Had a drunken, hot-headed classmate been chosen to face the gun, I'm not sure how it would have ended. But being able to slow down the encounter between myself and the gunman with some reasoning and non-aggressive movements bought us just enough time. Sirens and flashing blue lights caused the uninvited party guests to flee.

I still think about how many lives would have been ruined if this situation had gone another way. Most, if not all, involved were good young men at heart—they were just making foolish decisions fueled by alcohol. If it hadn't been for the regatta and my late arrival, I too may have been drunk and unable to offer the clear-minded "one hand" that helped break up the fight.

COMPELLED TO CARE

While writing this book, I received an email from a friend and Maritime alum. Titled "One Hand," it was sent to forty or so individuals in our cohort. It was an update on the family of our fellow teammate who had passed away several years ago. He'd valiantly fought against insidious cancer raging throughout his body. As is too often the case, his battle depleted the family's financial resources.

The author of the email remained in close contact with our friend's widow. When he'd asked how she and the kids were faring, she made an off-hand joke about coming home to a freezing house. This remark led to deeper questioning and the discovery that she and her family faced delinquent bills, leading to a lack of heating in their home.

Our friend's widow didn't ask for help; in fact, she resisted it. But our culture, bond, and love for our former classmate compelled us to step in and have his family's back. The group contributed over eight thousand dollars in less than a week.

In addition to the extraordinary results I've seen when individuals on a team use their unique talents to accomplish great goals, I'm struck with the positive psychological impact of knowing you are not alone in this world.

I've come to realize two things about myself. First, the experiences I had at an early age—from being bullied to witnessing the effect of harsh words on others—have been fuel for my desire to extend the one-hand principle. Second, because I'm personally driven to support others at all costs, I am not only disappointed when I don't see others moved to similar action—I get upset.

Helping isn't always easy, but one hand taught me that life is about caring for others. It's not about me; it's about the team. Phil Jackson writes, "Good teams become great ones when the members trust each other enough to surrender the 'me' for the 'we.'"[3]

– CHAPTER 4 –

LOVE
AND
STANDARDS

"Excellence implies striving for the highest standards in every phase of life."
—John W. Gardner

Two of my most life-changing events occurred during my years at Maritime. First, and most importantly, was my introduction to Stephanie Vinciguerra. A visiting friend showed me a wallet-sized photo of a beautiful brunette who lived near my hometown and told me that I needed to meet her. I was more than willing.

As soon as I was able to return for the summer, a double date at a restaurant across the border in Canada was arranged. It went *very* well, and I found myself completely hooked. That date grew into a three-year courtship and the most loving, impactful relationship of my life. I had no concept of the trust, support, and sacrifice Stephanie would demonstrate to me again and again in our years together. I just knew then—like I know now—that I was in love!

NOT JOINING THE NAVY

The other pivotal moment happened my junior year at Maritime when navy recruiter Lieutenant Andrea Jabuski walked into my nuclear engineering class one morning.

Usually, students at merchant marine schools transition into, well, the merchant marine. It wasn't my plan originally to end up in the navy. My dad had served for two years in the navy long before I was born. His feelings about his service were lukewarm at best. Looking back at my own enlistment, I would say that it happened almost by accident.

Lieutenant Jabuski came to tell us about the Nuclear Propulsion Officer Candidate program (NUPOC). Approximately one-third of all nuclear officers in the navy come from the NUPOC program, another third from the Naval Academy, and another third from ROTC. Jabuski waxed on about the financial gains of joining the nuclear navy and spoke of signing bonuses, nuke bonuses, and junior enlisted pay. In return for these benefits, we would have to agree to five years of service, including eighteen months of rigorous classes. It sounded good, but something didn't seem right. It felt like Jabuski was trying to sell us oceanfront property in Idaho.

After class, she found me in the hallway with my best friend, Eric Stolzenberg. The lieutenant invited us to visit Naval Station Norfolk, where we could get a taste of what she was offering, including access to the officer's club. It sounded like a time-share pitch to me, but Eric thought it was a great idea.

"Come on," he urged repeatedly. "Nothing is going on that weekend, and the trip is free!"

"Eric, I am not joining the navy. No way."

But Eric was right about the weekend being open, so I finally agreed to go—with the caveat that I was *not* joining the navy.

When we arrived, we were given two tours, one of an aircraft carrier and one of a submarine. The aircraft carrier was impressive, with its mammoth, imposing structure and incredible inner workings. But if I were assigned to a carrier, I would be a small fish swallowed up in a huge pond. The idea didn't spark excitement.

Stepping into the submarine was different.

The expertise and passion of the officer who gave us our submarine tour that day ignited the enthusiasm I didn't have on the aircraft carrier. As we walked through the ship, he recounted one thrilling tale after another.

He told stories about covert operations and going behind enemy lines. Missions of national security were just a part of his routine. The silent service he described brought me to the edge of my proverbial seat. He had pride in his work, the navy, and his fellow sailors.

It just got better as the officer talked about the camaraderie of a ship. The close quarters for extended periods created a sense of family, who—despite the solemnity of their missions—enjoyed pranks and good-natured fun. That really sang to me.

However, there were several significant problems with life on a submarine, including no communication with loved ones, and no fresh air or light for days on end. That part sounded awful. Besides, my Maritime training and experience was on a surface ship. This was much different.

Movies at the time focused on how prestigious it was to be a navy pilot. But that weekend, I learned that the nuclear navy is a quiet, somewhat nerdier group that is just as prestigious. This small select lot is trained to the highest technical standards . . . that is, if they manage to pass their classes. The attrition rate of this program is high. If I were accepted to Nuclear Power School, I'd be committing to an incredibly rigorous process and all of the mental push-ups it would entail.

My feelings against joining the navy switched that weekend. I began to weigh the options. Serving on a submarine sounded romantic, but the surface navy seemed to have fewer downsides. I called Stephanie and asked, "What do you think about me joining the navy?" She wasn't thrilled with the idea, but she must have heard some excitement in my voice. She encouraged me to go ahead. It was advice that would affect her life as much as it did mine.

Two years later, Stephanie would put aside her desire to pursue a master's in art history and agree instead to go with me to Kings Bay, Georgia. It would be the first of many moves and many sacrifices she would make on my behalf.

EARNING LUNCH

One of my favorite sayings is "there is no free lunch." Nothing drove this point home more than the NUPOC process. Before being officially accepted into the program, I had to be interviewed by Naval Reactors' personnel, the people who actually designed the nuclear reactor and equipment in plants on these vessels. I had to be well studied if I even hoped to move on to the next step. As I was ushered into Admiral Bruce DeMars's office, I was a bundle of nerves, sweaty palms and all. He fired a few reactor theory questions at me and then concluded simply, "Welcome to the program."

In the fall of my senior year, a new movie changed my perspective. *The Hunt for Red October* was a Cold War masterpiece full of spy missions, technical marvels, and the ever-cool Sean Connery. What was not to like? I found its intrigue and excitement so appealing that I decided to change my trajectory to submarines. I wanted to command a 688-class submarine just like the character Captain Bart Mancuso of the USS *Dallas*. I wanted to be a part of the teamwork and camaraderie the movie brought to life.

After graduation and commissioning, I reported to Naval Nuclear Power Training Command (NNPTC). The training consisted of six months of classroom lectures, endless studying, and punishing assessments. I passed, but I definitely could have done better.

The next six-month school, the Nuclear Power Training Unit (NPTU) in Ballston Spa, New York, was a command known as "prototype" that trained students on an actual reactor plant with hands-on exercises. Maritime had prepared me well for these types of activities, but the schedule was grueling. The hours were long, and the shifts changed weekly, from days to nights and back again.

The last school I had to attend before reporting to the USS *West Virginia* was Submarine Officer Basic Course (SOBC) in New London, Connecticut. This twelve-week course taught everything about submarines, from safety to seamanship.

By the end of these three exhaustive schools, I felt that I had definitely earned my lunch.

ADMIRAL RICKOVER

It was in Nuclear Power School that I first learned about the nuclear navy standards, which were created and rigidly upheld by Admiral Hyman G. Rickover. "The Father of the Nuclear Navy," Rickover's philosophy would come to influence my own throughout my entire career.

Before Rickover, the culture standards in the navy were to do what you're told, never ask questions, never challenge superiors, and hide problems.

He changed the culture in the nuclear navy because he knew the old ways would not sustain the safety critical to nuclear operations. He created a framework for initiative, construction, testing, and safety that the nuclear navy and hundreds of other organizations still utilize today.

An immigrant from Poland, Rickover earned an appointment to the Naval Academy at age eighteen and graduated in 1922. He served on traditional shipboard assignments and continued his education, earning an advanced degree in engineering. Eventually, he would become a four-star admiral. After World War II, he was selected to help design a nuclear electric generating plant.[4] Rickover understood the potential advantages of harnessing that same nuclear technology to fuel a variety of naval vessels, particularly submarines.

A nuclear submarine could remain concealed under the polar ice cap or in a strategic operating area without coming to periscope depth for weeks.

This ability for a ship to remain at sea for years without the need to refuel would enhance national security and give the United States Navy an enormous strategic advantage. Not everyone agreed with Rickover's vision, but he remained undeterred.

The work to develop, test, perfect, and maintain nuclear power seemed like a thankless job initially, but those who did it paved the way for a revolution in naval power. As Rickover overcame the initial pushback from the brass, he assembled teams from the top Naval Academy graduates who fought to interview with him for the coveted positions.

Rickover required that everyone who worked for him adhere to the same high standards of excellence he demanded of himself. His brash nature grew from his refusal to tolerate anything less than perfection. He knew that one accident could end the entire nuclear program. They had no room for error. Despite his rough demeanor, he cared about the men and women who worked with him toward a common goal, and he consistently risked his own back for the sake of those who served alongside him.

The admiral didn't care for ribbons, medals, or rank. He didn't mind what those above him in the chain of command thought of him or if other engineers considered him a mad scientist.

Rickover pushed his agenda with the navy brass, the American Congress, defense contractors, and old-school thinkers. He had no tolerance for inefficiency, cut corners, compromised safety, or apathy. He chastised others for asking insufficient questions and told them the questions they should be asking.

Many followed Rickover and carried his ethos throughout their entire careers. Tales of his personality and eccentricities are legendary among submariners. They speak of him as soldiers speak of George Patton or William T. Sherman. They loved or hated him, but critically, they trusted him.

INFAMOUS INTERVIEWS

Character was paramount to Rickover. To ensure every person entering the nuclear propulsion program was a person of integrity, Rickover, as the director of Naval Reactors, interviewed each prospective ensign himself. His interviews were notoriously difficult.

One officer I came to know shared with me his firsthand experience with the fabled admiral. When the officer was a midshipman in his junior year of the Naval Academy, he applied for the nuclear propulsion program. During the interview, Rickover perused the midshipman's grades and asked him if he would bring them up his senior year.

"Yes, sir!" the young man promised, convincing Rickover to accept him into the program.

The midshipman completed his senior year, entered the nuclear propulsion program, and progressed to the position of lieutenant. Three years later, the same man sat for his exam to become an engineer. The exam included another interview with Rickover and his subjective assessment of the officer's readiness.

"Lieutenant, are you a man of your word?" Rickover began abruptly.

"Yes, sir—of course, I am. I'm an officer in the US Navy!" the lieutenant replied.

Rickover pulled out the officer's transcripts from the Naval Academy. Then, mentioning the specific date of the lieutenant's initial interview three years earlier, Rickover said, "On this day, you promised you'd bring your grades up senior year. Your grades went down. Get out of my office!"

It wasn't a good sign. The lieutenant was stunned that Rickover would remember their conversation from so long ago and that he'd care about Naval Academy scores years after the lieutenant had graduated. The officer went home, not knowing whether he'd passed or failed the exam. He checked in every day to find out, but after three months of waiting for an answer, the lieutenant learned that Rickover had failed him. Rickover apparently doubted the lieutenant's integrity and resolve. He wanted to see if the officer would have the grit to return and retest.

At the time the officer told me his story, he was the captain of a submarine. So, he had indeed had the tenacity to sit for the engineering exam again. He never forgave Rickover, though. I was surprised by the level of bitterness the lieutenant harbored toward the admiral after so many years. Perhaps the initial failure had slowed the lieutenant's career, or maybe the emotional pain and embarrassment continued to linger. Despite the lieutenant's resentment, I'm sure he never forgot Rickover's difficult lesson on keeping his word.

Former president Jimmy Carter also suffered through a typical Rickover interview and described it this way:

> "How did you stand in your class at the Naval Academy?" Rickover asked.
>
> I swelled my chest with pride and answered, "Sir, I stood fifty-ninth in a class of 820!" I sat back to wait for the congratulations—which never came.
>
> Instead, the question: "Did you do your best?"
>
> I started to say, "Yes, sir," but I remembered who this was . . . I finally gulped and said, "No, sir, I didn't always do my best."

He looked at me for a long time, and then turned his chair around to end the interview. He asked one final question, which I have never been able to forget—or to answer. He said, "Why not?"[5]

Though Rickover's contemporaries had mixed feelings about him, they completely bought into his way of doing things. Vice Admiral E.P. Wilkins, inaugural commander of the USS *Nautilus* (SSN-571), summed up Rickover this way: "There's a part that's good, there's a part that's bad, and there's a part you wouldn't believe."[6]

Rickover's speech to the Columbia University School of Engineering in 1982 captured his thinking perfectly: "A good manager must have an unshakable determination and tenacity. Deciding what needs to be done is easy, getting it done is more difficult. Good ideas are not adopted automatically. They must be driven into practice with courageous impatience."[7]

Rickover didn't simply have good ideas. He had great ones. He remained undauntedly committed to them throughout his sixty-three years of naval service. No other American has served that long in the armed forces.

As the oldest and largest nuclear organization in the world, America's nuclear navy has the best safety record of any industry, according to *Forbes*.[8] There hasn't been a single accident among more than two hundred reactors in seventy years of operation. Impeccable training allows mere teenagers to operate highly complex reactors.

Other nations have experienced accidents with the development of dozens (and now hundreds) of nuclear-powered ships and land-based energy-producing plants. Some mistakes had devastating effects that still remain. Yet, the American nuclear navy has never had a mishap. Not one! That's the outcome of the culture of excellence Rickover cultivated through high standards, accountability, and courageous impatience.

I would learn much more about Rickover in the years that followed and would incorporate his standards of high reliability into industries beyond the navy. Unfortunately, as I finished power school and prepared for duty aboard the USS *West Virginia* (SSBN-736), I was on the cusp of learning a discouraging lesson. Despite rigorous training, certain commands didn't uphold the culture or all of the standards Rickover advocated for. Making no room for a "questioning attitude," some captains ruled instead with fear and intimidation.

— CHAPTER 5 —

THE PROBLEM WITH FEAR

"Leadership is solving problems. The day soldiers stop bringing you their problems is the day you have stopped leading them. They have either lost confidence that you can help or concluded that you do not care. Either case is a failure of leadership."

—COLIN POWELL

Fear is an onslaught of emotions that floods our senses when faced with a real or imagined event. It triggers biological sensations, prompting us to fight, flee, or freeze. Experts have categorized fear into five distinct areas and organized these into a pyramid resembling Maslow's great hierarchy of basic needs.[9]

At the base of the fear pyramid is extinction. This one is self-explanatory: we don't want to die or risk death by being at the edge of a cliff. Right along with that is the fear of mutilation. Again, it's about a threat to our physical bodies.

Moving up, the next fear is a loss of autonomy. As humans, we are tightfisted with control. While this fear can involve physical constraint—like what claustrophobics experience—it is more commonly manifested in relationships. Institutions like the military, for example, create hierarchical societies that impose restrictions and regulations. Some people find comfort in these types of relationships, while others feel stifled by cultures of authority.

A LOOMING LEADER

While I don't like to be told what to do all the time, as an ensign in the navy, I quickly grew accustomed to receiving directives. Obviously, the more junior you are, the more orders you take, and the fewer you give. As a people pleaser, I was happy to lay aside my personal desires for those of someone else, or for the good of the group. But I was also comfortable taking the lead and giving orders.

I don't feel stifled by the fear of losing autonomy, but I know it is a trigger for many people. Organizational psychologists tell leaders that giving subordinates control—or even a sense of it—ignites psychological well-being and creates better outcomes.[10] By providing at least a sense of control among your reports, you help reduce their fear. It's good for people.

The final categories of fear fall mostly in the relationship realm. Separation, the fourth fear, is the fear of abandonment, rejection, and exclusion. At the top of the pyramid is ego death, the fear of shame, disapproval, and loss of integrity or worthiness.

As I approached my first submarine assignment, I felt the flood of emotions associated with fear, but I was also extremely excited. I was about to report to a ballistic missile submarine, also known as a "boomer." Boomers are Cold War behemoths, 550 feet long—the length of almost two football fields. They are an essential component of the nuclear triad (aerial bombers, intercontinental ballistic missiles, or ICBMs, and ballistic missile submarines) that serve to deter war. The boomers are the most sustainable and survivable of the three weapons because they are stealthy and can hide in strategic locations for long periods of time, waiting to be called into action. ICBMs and bombers can't mask their positions.

My first commanding officer stood six feet six inches tall and seemed to weigh in excess of 250 pounds. He was a giant of a man with an even larger head.

As a child, one of my favorite Christmas movies was Rankin and Bass's Claymation *Santa Claus Is Comin' to Town*. The first time I saw my commanding officer, he immediately reminded me of the movie's villain, Burgermeister Meisterburger. Burgermeister was a curmudgeon of a mayor who hated toys and banned them in the village. It turned out my new captain's personality and appearance matched the character's.

Long before I joined the *West Virginia*, the commanding officer had been dubbed "MFB," which stood for something unmentionable. I'll never forget the day I first witnessed him earn that unmentionable description.

I had reported to the USS *West Virginia* (SSBN-736) as a young, twenty-three-year-old naval officer ready to do great things for submarine warfare. I served as the chemistry/radiological control assistant and communications officer. I also aspired to become an officer of the deck quickly. The first step was to qualify as engineering officer of the watch.

After passing a rigorous process, I was allowed to serve as the officer in charge of the nuclear reactor and propulsion plant. In the event our submarine needed to evade an enemy torpedo or quickly maneuver to avoid a collision, my job was to facilitate and maximize the continuity of reactor output to ensure survival. If the ship experienced flooding, I'd direct casualty efforts to ensure we didn't lose the ship. We ran intense reactor plant drills to prepare for life-or-death decision-making, especially in a time of war.

Our commanding officer, a former engineering plant officer himself, micromanaged these drills in an overbearing manner. His imposing frame lorded over us, and his critical eye searched for the slightest mistake. We expected him to unleash an explosive tirade at any moment. His presence created a sense of fear. He didn't trust us, and we didn't trust him.

At the time, I thought his presence aft was a normal part of the procedure. But, in my twenty-seven years of submarine experience that followed, I never saw another captain in the engine room during drills. The CO *should* be at the front of the ship, in the control room, ready to offset any errors the crew in the engine room might make that could cause a loss of propulsion.

The "box" or "maneuvering" is the eight-by-six-foot command-and-control area for the reactor and propulsion plant. The small, enclosed room could be quickly pressurized in the event of a steam line rupture. This would allow critical operations in the reactor to continue and provide protection to the four watch standers working in the propulsion spaces—the electrical operator (in charge of the electrical distribution and turbine generators), the throttleman (in charge of controlling steam to the main engines), the reactor operator (in charge of controlling the reactor), and the engineering officer of the watch (supervising the operations). Additionally, two others were present to assess the watch standers and monitor for safety.

During drills, MFB would wedge himself into the already cramped space, behind the reactor operator and in front of the engineering officer of the watch. Not only did his presence make the watch standers jittery, but his gigantic body also blocked critical information on the control panels. It felt like he raised the temperature of the confined space by several degrees.

A week before a drill, the engineer asked me if I was ready to serve as the engineering officer of the watch under instruction. I eagerly told him I was up for the task. I would be fine if the drill were to go without complications, but I was not ready to handle any deviation from the script or any fallout that would occur if I weren't perfect.

Early the next morning, I stationed myself in the box in preparation to run my first major drill. As I settled in, a massive form materialized just outside the box through the small viewing window. It was, of course, MFB.

He grunted, "Entering."

My anxiety spiked as I acknowledged his movement: "Entering, aye, sir."

The drill was to simulate a seawater leak into one of the vital ship systems. An adverse event such as this is called a "casualty." Shortly after the first drill began, a second-class petty officer made a small mistake while monitoring an alarm that would identify the source of the leak. As a result, the drill stalled. While all aspects of the drill were my responsibility, I'm not sure the most seasoned watch stander would have been able to prevent this error.

Suddenly, a roar burst from the top of MFB's lungs: "Fix your team, Engineer. This is unsatisfactory!" He pointed at the second-class petty officer who was also in the box, "You're not doing your damn job. Rerun the fucking drill!" His response was visceral.

The engine room vibrated as his bellow filled the box. Nothing in my training had prepared me for this kind of response from a leader.

As the team reset the drill, I could feel the quick pounding of my heart throughout my body. With the reset complete, I picked up the microphone to inform the engine room watch standers outside the box of the drill casualty indications.

I was acutely aware of how the delay had thinned MFB's patience—which was low to begin with. My hand shook noticeably as I brought the microphone up to my mouth. Then, as if someone else had control of my voice, it happened: the wrong command bubbled out. Before I finished the sentence, I knew I had screwed up.

Time stood still. Slowly and menacingly, MFB turned his head. His facial expression morphed from shock to rage. "Stop the damn drill!" He screamed louder than I had ever heard a human being scream before. The sound reverberated off the walls.

I froze in "standby and receive" mode.

He peered down at my five-foot-ten frame from his six-foot-four vantage point and positioned his reddened face within inches of mine. His nostrils flared and his brow furrowed. His meaty finger pointed at my nose as he reached deep into his diaphragm and roared, "You're not fucking ready. Get the hell outta here!" His spit sprayed my face.

When I say I pissed my pants a little, it's not hyperbole. He scared me that much.

The lesson that stayed with me was more about the culture of fear MFB created than any technical aspects of the job. When MFB lost control of his emotions that day—as he had on so many others—he also lost respect. We were all aware of his lack of emotional intelligence, and we knew we couldn't count on him to have our backs at the cost of his own.

Unfortunately, his behavior triggered ego-death fear for his crew: the fear of shame and disapproval. We operated in a way that subconsciously avoided situations that induced that fear. Instead of seeking the tutelage of our leader—the one who was in the position to teach and guide by example—we dodged interactions as much as possible.

It's unfortunate that this leadership style is common and has achieved a measure of success. People serving under it learn what to do to improve their skills just enough to avoid repetition of humiliating experiences. However, the damage this volatile style does to a culture negates any positive outcomes. Shaming only works in the short term. It doesn't inspire, it doesn't garner respect, and it doesn't build relationships. Over time, the presence of fear leads to egregious errors and a decline in performance.

A friend who served under MFB in another command told me that he was the only junior officer to continue in the navy from his tour. It's possible that MFB's previous ship didn't suffer many casualties, or adverse events, but the cost of turnover to the navy was immense—proof that leading by fear has long-term costs.

SCARED TO SPEAK

MFB's leadership style caused problems before I ever set foot on the *West Virginia*. About a year prior, a sailor had appendicitis and needed medical attention beyond the capacity of the medic on board. Shore command gave orders to medivac the sailor for immediate treatment. These included instructions to the nearest port for extrication and medical transport.

The officer of the deck and the radiomen initially missed the message that gave their destination because it came in with a long list of other messages. The orders sat for several hours until the changing of the watch standers, when several sailors read the message and realized the submarine had been on the incorrect course for hours.

Who was going to tell the captain of this error? Fear of his wrath was immense. As the story goes, a debate arose as the men pointed fingers, attempting to determine the bearer of bad news.

"You do it."

"No way, man. You noticed it first."

"Yeah, but you are closer to the door."

"Forget it. MFB likes you better."

"But I had to talk to him already today. You've been under the radar all day. I bet you haven't even passed in his shadow."

"Nope. You know I avoid him at all costs."

"I guess it is rock, paper, scissors, then."

"You've got to be joking."

Their shipmate was in dire need, so someone had to bite the bullet.

MFB blew a gasket when he found out they were off course and behind schedule.

Once the submarine was turned in the right direction, the commander ordered, "All ahead flank!"

It is a command reserved for situations of imminent danger, and it isn't taken lightly.

While all hands worked to get the submarine to maximum speed in the shortest amount of time, an engine room watch stander noticed a lube oil cooling issue—the cooler outlet temperature was one degree above the specified limit. The watch stander obtained permission from the engineering officer of the watch to shift to the standby cooler, which would continue to supply lube oil to the massive submarine's main engines, then proceeded to make the change without supervision. Neither he nor anyone else stopped to question the ramifications of conducting the necessary procedure while the ship traveled at maximum speed. The crew was more scared about telling MFB the temperatures were off and incurring his wrath than about the consequences of shifting coolers under the current conditions. Their anxiety left no room for critical thinking.

The chain of command was on edge, the fear of speaking up pervasive. Even senior officers tiptoed around MFB. A questioning attitude is essential to the operation of nuclear submarines, and the navy drills this attitude into all submariners' heads from their earliest moments in training. Under MFB, that freedom to question was missing. Not only were sailors scared to speak up, they were also apathetic toward the responsibility of keeping the ship safe. They skipped checks and balances, stifled their curiosity, and turned a blind eye to the work of others. The crew didn't care for the ship because they felt the command didn't care for them. Hallmarks of a safety culture were missing because the commander created no psychological safety for the crew.

The inexperienced watch stander in the engine room neglected to verify there was lube oil in the standby cooler. If he had, he would have discovered there was none. The lack of oil caused the failure of one of the two engines. The lack of supervision and guidance led to the disastrous mistake that cost the navy six million dollars to repair and over three months of a national strategic asset tied to a pier.

An investigation and a root cause analysis were conducted in order to understand what happened and to avoid a repeat of the error. The lack of oversight, the crew that did not speak up, and the generalized indifference were all issues that led directly back to MFB's leadership style. There was no doubt—the root cause of the mistake was the toxic culture.

SHIFTING THE BLAME

Soon, I had more MFB stories of my own. In some, I was the unfortunate soul who caught his wrath; in others, I was a witness.

Submarines are not submerged 100 percent of the time at sea. There are moments when it is necessary to cruise with the topside exposed, giving the ship sight to the surface and surrounding conditions. During these times, sailors alternate shifts to stand watch. Those on duty use the ship-wide communication system to expedite reporting and communication. Everyone on board can hear the conversation that transpires between the watch and the captain.

One time, we were cruising above the water on the outskirts of a hurricane. The two individuals assigned to watch were fully exposed to the weather as they perched on the sail (the high tower on a sub). In adverse conditions, the watch can shift to the control room to protect sailors from hazardous waves.

The weather worsened and became dangerous. The watch called down to the captain, requesting permission to shift the watch below decks. The quick response was an emphatic "no." This happened more than once. The sailors practically begged to go below decks. The response stayed the same, but MFB's impatience and irritated tone increased with each request.

Moments after a repeated plea was denied, a rogue wave shattered a plexiglass windshield and threw the two sailors against the metal hull of the ship. The men, harnessed to the ship, were saved from being cast overboard, but not saved from the force of the wave which threw them against the hard surface of the sail.

Their injuries finally forced the CO to allow the sailors to go below. They were taken to the medic room, where medics tended to their swollen, aching bodies. Between the two of them, they received twenty stitches.

MFB blamed the control room watch supervisor for not recommending moving the watch and clearing the bridge. He told the officer he should have recognized the danger by the "whooshing sounds of the wind" entering the tunnel that connects the bridge to the control room.

It was ludicrous that the firsthand account of the bridge watch standers was not enough for MFB to bring the men down out of danger. He did not own his poor decision. Instead, he shifted the blame, berated the young man before him, and literally threw the first book he could grab at the officer.

With MFB, these types of stories were all too common. As a result of the fear-based culture he created, the ship and its operations were substandard, and the risk of a catastrophic accident was great.

I saw firsthand the impact of humiliation on a team. I watched the sense of autonomy wane and the dejection it created. Like the sailors on the sail in bad weather, men even harbored fears of mutilation and extinction because they did not believe their leader had their best interests at heart.

GAME CHANGER

After my first patrol, the submarine had a change in management. Conditions under the new commanding officer were much better; his predecessor had set a low bar. However, with the accumulation of prior events, my desire to stay in the navy had waned. After a particularly grueling day, I returned home and told my wife, "Do *not* let me stay in the navy one more day than I have to. Promise me!"

Then a game changer came on the scene—our new executive officer, Mike McKinnon. He was joyful, approachable, and caring, with a great sense of humor.

A naturally slender guy, McKinnon earned the love and attention of the cooks. They kept him constantly supplied with cookies for the eighty or so days we were underway during his first patrol with us. When we returned to home port and it was time to change from his "poopie suit" (the blue polyester coveralls worn at sea) into his khaki uniform, McKinnon found the fitted khakis pretty snug.

He came into the control room as we were entering the port. He bent over to grab a book and, as he did, a strained button popped off his tight shirt and skipped across the metal deck, making plinking sounds as it bounced. McKinnon looked around sheepishly, wondering who had witnessed this event, and caught my eye. We both burst into laughter. "My wife is going to kill me!" he said.

In addition to his humor, which we badly needed, he shared sea stories that made us think submarine service might not be so awful. He worked to get us the awards we'd earned and made phone calls to help us secure our next assignments. He was a model of what a navy leader should be. He showed us love.

In fact, McKinnon convinced me that my next assignment should be instructing at Nuclear Power School in Orlando, Florida. It was a chance for both Stephanie and me to earn our master's degrees, and it offered an amazing opportunity for me to shape new leaders. The only problem was the assignment required me to sign a contract to do my department head tour on another submarine. It was a tough decision, especially since my words to my wife—"Do *not* let me stay in the navy one more day than I have to"—still rang in my head. But, thanks to McKinnon's positive influence, those words weren't ringing as loudly.

I went forward with the power school assignment. I honored the pain of my tour as a junior officer, knowing that I had grown from the experience. My tenure on the *West Virginia* fueled my desire to protect others and to lead in the best way possible. I was on the verge of learning what leading with love really meant.

Part Two:
Invaluable Lessons
of
Leadership Styles

— CHAPTER 6 —

AWAKENING

"A leader is someone who helps improve the lives of other people or improve the system they live under."

—Sam Houston

My time teaching at the NNPTC afforded me the opportunity to pursue my master's degree in engineering management at the University of Central Florida (UCF). During the day, I taught classes on the principles of science and engineering, design, construction, operations, and maintenance of naval nuclear propulsion plants. At night, I became a student.

TEACHING AND ENCOURAGING

I loved teaching. It was a lesson in leadership like no other. It humbled me and helped me to understand that leadership is about giving others the opportunity to shine and grow.

Prospective nuclear officers would begin their journeys at NNPTC, and I would help them navigate these treacherous waters. Power schools throws so much material at their students that we call it "drinking from a firehose." If a student doesn't study efficiently, there is no way to keep up. If they don't engage in lectures, absorbing and understanding the material will be almost impossible. Usually, students arrive before sunrise and leave well after sundown, even in the summer. It can be a time of true misery and fear for some.

I wasn't too far out of power school myself, so the sheer pain of it was fresh. When my students felt hopeless, I wanted them to see that success was possible. I told sea stories and tried to inject excitement and awe into my lessons. I wanted my students to appreciate the value and outcomes of nuclear navy standards the way that I did.

A FRIENDLY ANTAGONIST

I can't look back on my instructing days without thinking of Jeff Zeuner. Jeff was a year older than me and served as my unofficial mentor. He was brilliant, and I felt drawn to his love for mischief.

His competitive nature triggered mine, and we were off to the races—figuratively and literally. Jeff convinced me to run my first marathon with him at Disney World.

He was caring and made it fun when we trained together, but on game day, he became a different person. Beating me was his primary goal. He seemed to know how to get under my skin, but that only made me more determined.

During the marathon, Jeff pulled ahead and slowly increased his lead. He finished two minutes before me, about four seconds faster per mile.

The following week, whenever Jeff and I walked together in the halls, he'd look at his watch, count out four seconds, and say, "If you had just run that much faster per mile, you would have beaten me." That fueled our friendly lifelong competition. We've gone head-to-head on everything from cribbage to HORSE basketball to Ironman competitions. He even designed a trophy he named "The Z and B Cup" (putting his initial first, of course) that we pass back and forth to the latest victor.

A friendly antagonist, Jeff taught me the value of hard work, encouragement, and especially competition.

The unlikely combination of Rickover's methodology and Jeff's influence informed my teaching and fed my leadership style. My responsibility for preparing the next generation of nuclear submarine sailors humbled me. I cared for them and wanted them to feel the excitement of being part of the nuclear navy before a tyrannical command, like the one I'd experienced as a JO (junior officer), could crush their spirit. I wanted them to understand the reason behind our lifesaving high standards: compassionate care for one another.

FROM WORRY TO ACTION

Toward the end of this shore duty, I began to miss life aboard a submarine and the deep purpose that attracted me to the navy—service, sacrifice, and covert operations. I asked to be assigned to a submarine out of Pearl Harbor,

Hawaii. Stephanie and I didn't have children yet, and a few years in paradise sounded like a good idea.

Before serving as a department head (either as an engineer, a navigator, or a weapons officer), officers are required to go to another school in New London. This time it was five months in the Submarine Officer Advanced Course (SOAC). After completing school, I received verbal orders to the USS *Olympia* as a navigator (NAV) in Hawaii.

I experienced a whole new level of frustration when my orders began to change. Because of the smaller pool of officer-level candidates, assignments can be fluid. Verbal orders are really nothing more than a possibility of what might happen. My orders bounced to NAV on a ship based in San Diego and then to a weapons officer (WEPS) back in Pearl.

The changes made me anxious. I worried about the crew that I would join and feared getting another commanding officer like MFB. The unknown prompted me to invent and dwell on worst-case scenarios.

Fortunately, luck was on my side. Just a few weeks before receiving my final written orders, I had the chance to pick up some valuable intel in the head (bathroom), of all places.

Two officers were talking. I was mostly ignoring them, as is polite in such situations, but one line caught my attention: "I heard the guy set to relieve as navigator on the *Asheville* broke his leg. I'd give my left nut to work for Grooms again."

A commanding officer whom sailors and officers would fight to serve with? That was exactly what I was looking for! I didn't want to leave my circumstances to fate. If this Grooms guy, the CO of the *Asheville*, was so awesome, I would have to take control of the situation.

Armed with that beneficial intel, I sought out the detailer. Detailers are responsible for assignments and hold people's destinies in their hands. My detailer was a little reluctant to make the change after the multiple assignment shifts my class had gone through. He didn't want to do more juggling. However, I did my best to persuade him, and, at last, he relented and adjusted my assignment.

I didn't know it at the time, but he was providing me with the opportunity to learn from the best of the best. That single piece of information overheard during a bathroom break would change my career and my life. Unfortunately, a terrible personal tragedy overshadowed my good fortune.

SHATTERING NEWS

On a cool New England spring day, I was attending an attack center—a dark mock-up of a submarine control room where war scenarios are simulated—

when the director of sub school tapped my shoulder and asked me to step out into the hallway. As I stood in the musty, linoleum basement under the harsh fluorescent lighting, the director delivered the shattering news that my beloved father had taken his own life. I felt my knees buckle. In that instant, my entire reality shifted.

In addition to the pain of losing my dad, I experienced a wave of guilt and regret over the strained relationship that had developed between us in the previous years because of Mom's mental health.

Since my sophomore year in college, my mother had suffered from severe mental illness. She began a downward spiral of delusional and aggressive behavior. She refused professional assistance. For years, my father tried to placate my mother and attempted to build a happy life together in their newly retired state. But her illness was beyond his help, and it broke his heart.

My mother's disease made her behavior toward my wife unbearable. After Mom's repeated verbal abuse of Stephanie and unheeded warnings from me, I felt I had no choice but to cut ties with my parents.

Dad had always held family so dear. It was too much for him to see it in shambles.

I learned my dad had tried to call me shortly before he shot himself, but I hadn't been home. I was wrecked by the thought of that missed call and the possibility I could have done something.

I made the long, lonely trek from New London to Dunkirk, New York. The anguish of the drive was indescribable. Pain permeated every fiber of my body. I desperately wished to turn back time just enough to save my father. Once my wife was able to join me, I cried inconsolably. It was the only time I can remember crying in front of her.

THE REAL DEAL

I lost the focus and excitement my orders to the *Asheville* had initially brought. Heartache tainted the joy of our move to Hawaii and my transition to life aboard a new ship, but we did our best to move on. I buried the pain of the loss for the time being.

I received a little boost when a USS *Asheville* ballcap came in the mail before I left SOAC. As I planned to meet the submarine in Yokosuka, Japan, about midway through its deployment, I regained some of my excitement. A young JO, Jon Moretty, picked me up at the airport and brought me to The Sanctuary, a building on the base where submariners could escape the confines of their tiny spaces on board and enjoy a cold beverage or play pool.

Jon introduced me to my new captain, Bruce Grooms, and the executive officer, Lee Hankins.

"Captain, this is Lieutenant Roncska, the new navigator."

They both looked haggard from a long stint at sea. I wanted to make a good first impression and assumed they'd size me up.

After exchanging pleasantries, I said, "Captain, I really appreciate the ball cap. Made my week."

Grooms smiled at Hankins, a silent salute to acknowledge Hankins's efforts to make me feel welcome. The hat had been the XO's idea.

Instead of a stiff welcome, their casual demeanor set a tone that would prevail the entire time I was under their shared leadership. Their body language was open and inviting. I felt at home right from the start.

As I wandered around The Sanctuary, meeting my new shipmates and swapping sea stories, the legend of Grooms began to unfold. What the group shared about their most recent mission blew me away.

The *Asheville* had been charged with finding and tracking an adversary's submarine, a particularly desirable target.

Oftentimes on these missions, experts join the crew temporarily to aid in the search. An acoustics intelligence officer (ACINT) was riding the ship to lend his expertise in identifying sounds and differentiating between mechanical and environmental noises.

Grooms received an excited call from a crew member in the sonar room, exclaiming, "We got him, Captain!"

However, upon further review, the ACINT told the captain it wasn't their target. Grooms deferred to the expert, the *Asheville* moved on, and Grooms retired for the evening. He'd drifted off to sleep when a seventeen-year-old seaman knocked on his door, requesting permission to enter.

After the groggy captain invited the sailor in, the young man asked Grooms why he had decided to move on from tracking the enemy asset. The young man was sure that what he had heard was, in fact, their target. Grooms thanked the sailor and dismissed him, intending to return to bed. But after a moment of reflection, he decided to go back and track the sound.

His late-night visitor had been right. The crew of the *Asheville* was able to identify and monitor the enemy ship. Grooms probably looked like a hero to the higher-ups, but he made sure to recognize the young man who'd spoken up and convinced him to return.

I was astonished. Of course, I was aware that everyone on board a nuclear vessel was *supposed* to speak up if they saw something wrong. It was a training standard established by Admiral Rickover and one I myself had taught in Nuclear Power School. However, I had rarely seen it in action on my last submarine. I tried to imagine that same young man knocking on MFB's door and interrupting his slumber. Undoubtedly, MFB would have berated the sailor, and the results would have been drastically different.

I wanted to pinch myself. *Was this for real? Did my new captain actually value the opinions of others? Did he care enough about each crew member to hear their concerns and treat them with respect?* I was beyond thrilled at the thought of being part of his crew.

About three weeks later, I saw firsthand that Grooms led in a much different way than what I'd experienced before. He was definitely the genuine article.

COMPLIMENTS TO THE CHEF

Not every circumstance on a submarine presents a life-or-death situation. That doesn't mean small matters are not important, though. The trust Grooms built in seemingly insignificant instances could be relied on in more critical moments. The way he handled the following situation spoke volumes.

For sailors who are out to sea, quality food provides more than sustenance; it's life. Mealtimes are a welcome break during those long days and nights, and delicious food is good for morale. Every year, the navy honors the best galleys on ship or shore with the coveted Captain Edward F. Ney Award. The Ney, which recognizes excellence in food service management, sanitation, delivery, and overall performance, is a big deal to navy mess cooks. On the *Asheville*, I witnessed a masterclass in leadership as I watched the hardworking chefs prepare for the Ney Award inspection.

During our daily planning meeting, our supply officer (CHOP) informed Captain Grooms of the Ney team's scheduled arrival the next day and asked if he had time to meet with them. Without hesitation, Grooms replied, "Absolutely, clear my schedule."

Captain Grooms had noticed the extensive efforts of our head cook, Culinary Specialist First Class (CS1) Bobby Irish. CS1 Irish scrubbed the galley from top to bottom. He inventoried his stores and supplies and made sure he provided contingencies for unplanned circumstances. He trained on different methods and recipes so that he could deliver high-caliber meals. The love Irish had for the job, the crew, and the ship was reflected in the joyful way he did his work and the pride he took in the results. This love permeated his division.

Grooms realized that well-fed sailors perform better. He provided the mess crew with any resources they required and made himself available if there was a need he could fulfill. He took a genuine interest in the mess's preparations for the Ney team's inspection, but he didn't micromanage.

Shortly before the Ney team arrive, Grooms pulled Irish aside, looked him in the eyes, and thanked him for making sure the crew was well taken care of. He promised to let the inspectors know that the *Asheville* had the finest galley in the navy.

The Ney Award inspectors came and went. Despite Grooms's support, the *Asheville* wound up only a runner-up for the award. Irish was crushed. He'd wanted the honor for the entire ship, especially his commanding officer. He felt he had let down the crew.

Not long after receiving the bad news, Irish told me of the support Grooms had given him throughout the process. When the captain noticed Irish was taking the loss very personally, he laid a hand on Irish's shoulder and said, "I'm sorry we didn't get the Ney. I know you're disappointed, but you win that award every day in my book. What you do is critical to our mission, and we're lucky to have you."

Though the words didn't relieve Bobby Irish's sting of disappointment entirely, Grooms's compassionate response helped him see that his hard work did not go unnoticed. The cook continued his exemplary service under Grooms, and the entire crew benefitted.

SENDING A MESSAGE

Captain Grooms took pride in our vessel. He expected us to meet the highest of standards, keep vigilant, and always be prepared. While we kept the ship and our processes in top order, Grooms encouraged us to give extra effort as we readied for inspections.

Like the Ney award, Grooms believed that high marks on inspections were a testament to the sailors, not to himself. He was a visible presence, frequently sharing a kind word for the work being done. Grooms showed up to support, not interfere. He let us know he trusted us and gave us the latitude we needed to accomplish our tasks.

When *Asheville* went through an Operational Reactor Safeguards Exam (ORSE), we scored lower than Grooms anticipated—not a bad score, but not what he expected or felt the crew deserved.

During the post-inspection debrief, the inspectors gave a report indicating the ship's strengths and the areas they felt needed improvement. Grooms's disapproval of the inspectors' process and findings was clear. He walked out before the report was complete, sending a message of displeasure. Grooms didn't tell us about his actions, but two other *Asheville* officers who were present at the debrief told us how Grooms had spoken up to those in power on our behalf. His defense of our performance and honor didn't change the outcome of the exam, but they deepened our loyalty to him and further strengthened our culture.

Years later, I had the opportunity to ask Grooms why he'd walked out.

"It was about the crew," he said. "They worked really hard, and the grades did not reflect their performance."

Grooms explained that a couple of those involved in grading the inspection didn't get along and had used the situation to work out their grievances. Under the surface, it had been a political struggle, and Grooms wanted his opinion of the results made clear.

He also said that, looking back, he was somewhat embarrassed by his actions and would have been a bit more civil if given the opportunity to do it over. He said that his friend and mentor, Vice Admiral Al "the sailor's pal" Konetzni, had called him into his office shortly after the debrief and walked him back from the ledge. Grooms viewed Konetzni's advice to "let it go" and "move on" as invaluable.

Like his nickname indicates, Konetzni was known for the exceptional way he took care of sailors. I never had the opportunity to work directly for him, but I couldn't help but reflect on the snowballing benefit of his mentorship of Grooms for myself and many others. The full impact of a loving leader's actions extends far beyond what they will ever know.

Though Grooms may regret his reaction to a degree, I am still impressed by it. He showed us that he would stick up for his crew despite personal costs. It was clearly an act of love.

PEOPLE FIRST

Grooms cared for his team as much as he cared for his ship. One particular interaction with the captain made me realize the degree to which he valued my own well-being.

A ship in port has a regular Monday-through-Friday routine, with weekends off. The ship, however, can't be left unattended on the weekends. Much of the work continues, so crew members rotate weekend duty. As the operations officer, I was responsible for creating the schedule and overseeing the watch for duty stations.

One Sunday, while standing duty, I shared the weekend responsibilities with another officer. I was in the aft of the ship overseeing the reactor and engine room, and he was in the forward. On this particular day, we were extremely busy with required maintenance aft, but there wasn't much happening forward.

To give the officers some time home over the weekend, we would usually "single the duty"—one duty officer would take over both sets of responsibilities, allowing the other duty officer to leave the ship, usually by late morning. Even though it was my turn to go home, on this Sunday, I was too caught up in all the maintenance.

By early afternoon, I was just taking my first opportunity to use the head. As I passed the wardroom on my way, the phone rang. It irritated me. I had too much to do, and there weren't enough hands to get it all done. The others on board who typically answered the phone were busy too, so I picked it up.

"Good morning. This is the USS *Asheville*. This is a non-secure line. This is the navigator speaking. How can I help you?"

"*What* are you doing?" The voice on the line was gruff.

This man had the gall to call and demand a status update from me. *Who did he think he was?*

"Excuse me?" I said with more than a hint of attitude. I didn't have time for this.

"What are you doing?" came an even sterner response.

Then it hit me. I recognized the deep voice of the commander. It was Grooms!

"Captain?"

"Yeah. What are you doing?"

My mind was racing. *What did I do wrong? Did I overlook something? Did I not report something? Why was he mad?*

"Why haven't you called me yet?" he asked.

"Captain?" I was confused.

"Why haven't you called me to single the duty?"

"I was busy getting the maintenance done aft."

"Turn that over. There is not much going on in the forward. The forward duty officer can do that."

He was adamant: "Get home. Enjoy your time. It is a beautiful Hawaiian day. Stephanie is waiting for you. She doesn't see you enough. Go single the duty."

"Do you want to talk to the duty officer?" I asked.

"No."

"Do you need anything?"

"No, single the duty and get out of there. That's an order."

"Single the duty. Aye, sir."

"Great. Keep up the great work, NAV. Go enjoy your day, you deserve it. I really appreciate you."

The phone line went dead, and that's the last I heard from Grooms that day.

Not only had Grooms recognized the toll of the extra duty and prioritized my need for respite over the scheduled maintenance, he had also worried about me during his own free time. His simple phone call impacted me deeply. Grooms put people first. He cared about the well-being of his crew and understood the importance of time with family. He cared about *me*.

ROOM TO NAVIGATE

On board *Asheville*, I had the responsibility to ensure that the software for our message routing system (DPVS) was updated. This database validated our messaging system to ensure the routing of communications to the correct inboxes. It was important that the database was up to date, because the system did not flag incorrect addresses as "undeliverable." When sending a message, you were flying blind, trusting that the system was correct and messages were being routed appropriately.

When I asked the radioman if DPVS had been updated, he said the process had not yet begun.

"Okay, please make sure you have the latest software today."

"Aye, sir."

I checked back the next day and found the task had still not been done. I was more emphatic with my request and indicated I would expect completion the following day. On the third day, the radioman told me it had been done. I nodded, thanked the sailor, and moved on.

I didn't realize then how the DPVS updates would intertwine with another responsibility of mine: the dependent's day cruise. Grooms wanted to extend his appreciation to the families of his crew by providing them the opportunity to board the ship and experience life underway. Each member of the crew could invite loved ones to join us as we traveled between Pearl Harbor, Oahu, and Lahaina, Maui. Family members would fly in, board the sub, and partake in one of the legs of the journey. Many of the families would choose to stay at a local hotel a few days after to extend their time together.

I was to organize and oversee the event. This token of gratitude for the families was extremely important to Grooms, and I didn't want to let him down. It was an opportunity to show that I was a competent leader who could handle even minute details.

I was responsible for getting approval for the event, the navigational route, and docking at the port of Maui. Requests had to be made at least a month prior to the cruise in order for the needed processing and permissions to be granted.

I ensured all the requests were appropriately submitted to the Commander of Navy Region (COMNAVREG) days before leaving on a three-week mission that preceded the dependent's day cruise. We returned from the mission with just over a week to finalize preparations for the event. Following our mission debriefing, the squadron operations officer approached our navigation team.

"Hey, who's the navigator?" I was relatively new and still unknown. I looked at him and indicated my rank.

"Are you going on a dependent's cruise?"

"Yeah, I sent the request with all the details."

I showed him a copy of my requests. The officer looked over my submission and said, "You sent it to the wrong address. Is your DPVS up to date? You're not going to go. It takes a month's turnaround time for permissions. They never got your message, and you missed the window."

My heart sank. I was devastated by this news.

Not long after, I saw the captain walking off the pier and helping his wife into their car. I approached him gingerly and said, "Captain, we're having a problem with the dependent's day cruise. Just want to update you. I'm going to COMNAVREG. I'll call you tonight to let you know. But the dependent's cruise is in jeopardy."

His face dropped. I could see and feel his concern. But instead of yelling or firing off a lot of questions, he simply said, "Okay, let me know."

He was giving me leeway to attempt the rescue. I felt trusted, and I wanted to deliver.

I immediately got into my car and drove across the base to COMNAVREG. It was in an old World War II building that looked like a prop from a movie set. I spoke to the first individual I saw.

"Hey, are you the department that approves this?" I handed him a copy of the request I had attempted to send weeks before.

The officer scanned the document, "Yeah, that's us."

"I'm so sorry. I messed this up. Let me tell you what happened."

I briefly explained what went wrong and stressed the importance of the assignment.

The officer was so kind. "Not a problem. Let me help you. All I have to do is fax over a request to the port of Maui to see if all the logistics will work out. I'll do it right now."

I appreciated his kindness but worried the port of Maui would not be able to deliver without the proper notification time. I didn't have to wait long to find out.

As I was driving back, I got miraculous news.

"You are all set," the officer from COMNAVREG said. "It came back approved. You are good to go."

I was so relieved. I felt my tension ease and my shoulders relax. I would have good news to report. I eagerly called the captain, and his wife, Emily, answered.

Warm and caring, like her husband, she chatted with me for a few minutes before I asked if the captain was available.

"Oh! He's giving the kids a bath. Can I have him call you back?"

"No, I don't want to disturb him. Please just relay the message that the dependent's cruise is all set. We are good to go."

The following morning, I heard the dinging of the arrival bell and the signal that the captain was actively boarding. I quickly moved across the ship to meet Grooms as he entered his stateroom and sat down.

"Captain, did you hear?"

"Yeah, I heard," he said, glumly. I was confused by the disappointment in his tone.

"What's wrong?"

"Emily told me. It's canceled."

"No! It's on! I called to tell you that we are all set. Everything is worked out."

A pause. A quiet chuckle grew, and the captain's deep signature laugh filled the small space.

"Do me a favor. Never tell Emily anything ever again. She has a habit of messing with me, and she got me good. Great job, NAV. Keep up the good work."

Even when Grooms thought I had failed, he didn't shame me. He gave me room to navigate the problem. His words and actions didn't instill a fear of ego death or a feeling of unworthiness; rather, they empowered me. I learned to expect this kind of treatment from Grooms when an honest mistake was made. However, when clear standards were knowingly or carelessly violated, Grooms would get angry. Such actions put others at risk and triggered his guardian instinct.

I came down hard on the radioman who'd confirmed the software had been updated when, in fact, it hadn't been. I was frustrated by how close the lie had come to scuttling the dependent's cruise and disappointing many people I cared about. In retrospect, I wish I had extended the radioman more grace. I was still learning from Grooms, though, and my response to failure in others did begin to change over time.

A MODEL OF LEADERSHIP

Halfway through my second year on the *Asheville*, Captain Grooms and I attended a meeting with Captain Fred Dohse, the commodore of the squadron, to plan our future missions. As always, Grooms was excited about the challenge of another mission. But, when we sat down, the commodore turned to Grooms and said, "I'm sorry, Bruce, you're not doing this deployment."

A successful college football player in his junior year will often skip playing as a senior rather than jeopardize a career in the NFL. The commodore used the same reasoning in Grooms's case. A multitude of things could go wrong on a deployment, and the navy had bigger plans for the captain.

As we left the squadron building, a crestfallen Grooms turned to me and said, "Please don't say anything. I need to tell the crew in my own time." Even in the midst of his personal disappointment, Grooms was thinking about his men.

Today, I consider Admiral Bruce Grooms the most influential leader I've ever worked with. My experience under his command was all too short. In 1999, the navy awarded him the Vice Admiral James Bond Stockdale Award for Inspirational Leadership. Named after the man who showed undaunted leadership of fellow POWs during the Vietnam War, the Stockdale Award recognizes ethics, teaching, stewardship, and overall management of naval resources.

Grooms was also one of "The Centennial Seven"—the seven African Americans who commanded a submarine in the twentieth century. Before retiring, he donned three stars on his uniform as a vice admiral.

Military leadership may connote a screaming drill sergeant, a valiant officer lifting his sword to lead a cavalry charge, or a general delivering an empowering speech. Grooms did not reflect any of these stereotypes, yet he excelled. I knew that if I modeled his methods, I would be successful too. So much of my leadership style today has followed Grooms's blueprint.

Grooms treated us like family and built trust. His caring attitude and skills as a mentor more than warranted that comment I overheard in the head so long ago. Now I can echo the sentiment: "I'd give my left nut to work for Grooms again."

— CHAPTER 7 —
THE EROSION
OF
TRUST

"Take the long way. Do the hard work, consistently and with generosity and transparency. And then you won't waste time doing it over."

—SETH GODIN

The saying "All good things must come to an end" never felt truer to me than when Grooms left the USS *Asheville*. In time, the family culture that Grooms built faded, and eventually, the great results disappeared too.

The crew had cautious optimism about the incoming commanding officer, whom I will call Captain Fenwick. He was incredibly competent in the technical and tactical field, which earned our respect immediately. But he had a completely different approach to leadership, and our hope and trust eroded as his tour continued.

UNBRAIDING A CULTURE

I stood topside one morning, shortly into Captain Fenwick's command. A petty officer in charge of the deck division approached me, excited to show me an intricate lanyard he had gone to great efforts to create for the ship's pennant and flags. This crewmember, on his own, had learned to do the braiding and had paid for the material himself. I had to admit, the braiding was beautiful.

"Do you think the captain will like it?" he asked me eagerly.

"Absolutely!" I replied. I honestly couldn't see how the captain could be anything but impressed.

Moments later we heard the bell announcing Fenwick's arrival. The petty officer rushed to catch him before he descended into the ship.

"Captain! Do you have a minute?"

"Sure," Fenwick responded half-heartedly. Clearly, his mind and attention were not focused on the young sailor.

The petty officer proudly showed the captain his work.

"Huh. That's nice but could have used a different color," the captain said, smirking and walking away.

With that small comment, which Fenwick probably found insignificant or even funny, the captain revealed his lack of consideration for the sailor's feelings and effort.

It was demoralizing, and no one laughed. In fact, you could have heard a pin drop. It was the sound of a culture dying.

A MESS OF DAMAGE

Another example of the vast difference between our old and new command is the follow-up story of the Ney Award. Bobby Irish never wavered in running a pristine and high-performing galley. As the second Ney Award inspection neared, he cleaned, inventoried, trained, and strategized to perform even better than the last time.

At a planning meeting, the CHOP informed the captain of the upcoming assessment, exactly as he had done a year prior with Grooms. "Sir, the Ney inspection team is arriving tomorrow. Would you like to attend the inspection in brief?"

"No," Fenwick answered bluntly. He didn't appear to understand or care about the hard work of the culinary specialists.

The Ney inspectors came and went without much interaction from the captain. Again, the ship didn't win. Again, Irish felt that he had let everyone down.

"Sorry, better luck next time" was all the encouragement the captain had to offer.

When someone feels taken for granted, they will typically tell others. Irish freely shared his disappointment with the captain's level of support to anyone who would listen. News of Irish's experience spread throughout the ship like wildfire. The change in culture accelerated immediately as the story traveled. The incident marked a turning point in the wrong direction.

Captain Fenwick failed to provide appreciation through love the way that Grooms had. Grooms understood the difference between managers and leaders. Managers deal with tactics; leaders focus on people. Acclaimed speaker and author Simon Sinek says, "Leaders are not responsible for the results. Leaders are responsible for the people who are responsible for the results."[11]

The crew had established tight bonds and considered one another family. Irish's hurtful experience damaged us all. Each person who heard the story felt just as incensed as Irish, and the incredulity toward the experience fueled the retelling of it.

We knew the value of the mess crew, and we all expressed our gratitude for them. It probably provided some comfort, but not enough. There was only so much the rest of us could do to make up for the absence of command support.

DISRESPECT GOES FURTHER

The callousness of command and the worsening culture had a ripple effect that reached my own family. The ship had scheduled a post-deployment award ceremony, and I had been nominated for an award. My wife received notice of her required attendance, or "mandatory fun," as she termed it. Her special projects and job as a third-grade teacher kept her working long hours, and she was exhausted, but she went with a smile. Reason 1,001 that military spouses and children should be remembered and thanked for their service.

We arrived at a beautiful, open-air venue called Lockwood Hall in Pearl Harbor. During the buffet, Stephanie noticed that Bobby Irish and his team were serving us. This was supposed to be their celebration as well, and it didn't sit right with her that they had to work the event.

Feeling angry on Irish's behalf, Stephanie watched the ceremonies begin. Awards are passed out in ascending order of rank, and she waited as the list of officers was announced. When the XO's name was called before mine, Stephanie knew immediately that I had been passed over. The XO, only on board for a short time, had been responsible for ensuring everyone's awards were correctly processed. When it was his turn to receive an award, he puffed out his chest with exaggerated military pride.

This enraged Stephanie. She had been ordered to attend the ceremony, only to see someone else, for whom she had little respect, get an award while her husband was forgotten. The command's thoughtlessness and contempt of her time soured Stephanie on future events—and our navy experience in general.

I don't tell this story because I missed out on an award; it was an oversight that was rectified later. I share it because my wife's opinion of the command took a massive hit that day. It was not the mistake that infuriated her—mistakes happen—but rather the lack of consideration. My missing award should have been flagged, and the oversight communicated to us both before the ceremony. What's more, Irish and his team should have been enjoying the event rather than working it.

Respect can go a long way. Disrespect can go even further—in the opposite direction. The awards dinner caused my wife to disdain navy functions in a way she never completely overcame.

This event reinforced a lesson I'd learned under Grooms. To take care of my people, I had to take care of my people's people. To love my teams, I had to respect and honor their loved ones too.

UNSAFE TO SPEAK

I still had a long time to serve under Captain Fenwick. I attempted to keep "the Grooms way" alive, but it was difficult as I continued to witness culture-killing behavior. Once, we had an officer of the deck who needed to bring the ship within two hundred feet of the surface to correct a small mistake his watch team had made. He informed the captain of the error and asked when the captain would like to critique the minor incident.

"At the most inconvenient time possible," the captain said before walking away.

His response told the crew that reporting problems led to punishment.

Later, following a poor performance of the ship on an exam, a command climate survey was conducted. When reviewing the results, Captain Fenwick read aloud one of the anonymous comments that referenced himself: "It's clear that this is your ship, and not ours."

The captain's response? "You're damn right. Next comment."

I wish now that I had brought up my concerns about the deteriorating culture to the captain or XO. But I was still very junior and didn't feel like I could. When it comes to the safety of the reactor and the engine room, if something doesn't seem right, we have been drilled to speak up. That's one of the reasons the navy has its impeccable safety record. Outside of that environment, however, it's difficult to voice concerns when psychological safety is missing.

Mike Wilkerson, a former shipmate, reminded me recently of another psychologically unsafe incident Captain Fenwick had created. The USS *Asheville* was the second submarine to have a new sonar system installed. The system had many bugs and continued to crash. It was so bad that the first sub to receive the sonar had to pull in from an underway to have the system serviced.

After multiple attempts to fix our sonar, the command issued a letter of instruction (LOI) to Mike, the sonar technician. LOIs are never fun to get, but they are meant to give prescriptive actions to fix an issue. This command, however, seemed to give them punitively. The XO generated Mike's LOI, indicating "improper maintenance" on the sonar system. When Mike spoke to Captain Fenwick, he attempted to explain that the team had been doing the proper maintenance, but the new system was just not working correctly.

"Are you calling my XO a liar?" the captain barked.

Honestly, how can anyone feel safe speaking up when faced with a reaction like that?

Working for a leader who didn't recognize our value took its toll. A caring attitude would have encouraged the crucial, often difficult conversations that need to happen to build an excellent ship and team. Without it, we avoided confronting issues with the command and instead shared our outrage with each other. We weren't blameless, but it was the responsibility of the commanding officer to set the tone, coach us when needed, and hold everyone accountable for their respective part of the culture.

Captain Fenwick wasn't a bad person; he just didn't understand the magic of a strong culture or have the skills to maintain the stellar one he had inherited from his predecessor. Nor did he have the insight to appreciate psychological safety as a key ingredient of a great team. He didn't see how his actions eroded our trust.

DIRE STRAITS

On its way to join a battle group deployment, the *Asheville* transited a route through the Strait of Hormuz with Captain Fenwick at the helm.

In not-so-friendly territories, such as Iran, it is essential to be on high alert, so as not to create an international situation by unintentionally traveling outside of constrained parameters. The Strait of Hormuz is very narrow, and we were required to stay within the shipping lanes, all while being submerged. If needed, we could depart the lane under the innocent passage laws, which allowed us to travel within twelve miles of foreign territory. The laws and treaties, however, required us to minimize our time and proceed quickly through to the other side.

The water depth in the Strait of Hormuz can be as shallow as 160 feet. At that depth, there is little clearance for a submerged submarine from the keel at the bottom to the sail at the top.

To compound matters, the strait is extremely crowded with oil tankers and other vessels. Ships do not pass through in a single file, and the traffic is bidirectional. In addition to the depth and traffic patterns, the draft of other vessels—the depth between the waterline and their lowest point—is a huge safety issue for submarines. Some supertankers create a draft of fifty or sixty feet. In short, there's often not enough room.

Additionally, submarines have speed restrictions for certain water depths. The restrictions are in place to help in the worst-case scenario, in which the stern planes become jammed and the submarine finds itself headed for the ocean floor. A slower velocity will buy the sub time to react and correct. However, the speed restriction becomes problematic when ships approach from behind at a faster rate.

As we navigated through the strait, our pace was limited by the shallow depths, and it impacted our ability to stay out of the way of ships approaching from the rear. It was my job as the navigator to issue a track for the officer of the deck to follow in order to move through the tight space safely.

The officer of the deck detected a fathometer of a ship astern. The ping of the device used to measure ocean depth registered on our equipment loud and clear. Detection at such a high frequency indicated another ship was extremely close to us. The officer of the deck called, asking if he could deviate from our track.

"Absolutely," I answered immediately. "Come right. You are authorized to deviate from track."

Two minutes after our deviation, the submarine was shaken like a rag doll. We pitched up fifteen degrees and down twenty. Through the hull, we could hear a propeller of a supertanker above.

Cha, cha, cha, cha.

I stood in shock, with my eyes bulging. I heard myself gulp and realized we had barely dodged a bullet. Had that officer and I not trusted one another, had he not felt the psychological safety to suggest we move off track, we would have collided with the supertanker.

Though Captain Fenwick came to the control room immediately to receive an account of the near miss from the officer of the deck, the CO said little about it.

His silence about the incident continued when, after returning home a month later, he chose not to mention it during his end-of-mission report. To my knowledge, the navy didn't strictly require an accounting of such an event at the time, but sharing the intel would have undoubtedly served the best interests of the submarine community. Traveling the Strait of Hormuz was fairly new to our force. We could have saved other submarines from making the same mistake.

I look back and wish I'd had the hutzpah to ask my CO for permission to give the report myself. My inexperience laced with a culture-driven fear of vulnerability, kept me silent as well.

Several years later, the USS *Newport News* (SSN-750) attempted the same maneuver through the same waters. Directly over them, a supertanker's massive draft created the Venturi effect, propelling the submarine upward into the pressure vacuum. The sub collided with the underside of a tanker, causing millions of dollars in damage and lost time at sea for both ships. The CO was relieved of his duty, and the navy suffered international embarrassment. Scuttlebutt blamed a poor culture that fostered the fear of speaking up.

This unfortunate tale illustrates the importance of transparency at all costs. The navy should have celebrated our near miss on the *Asheville* and written a standard operating procedure to disseminate after our experience. That kind of learning and follow-up would have contributed to the operational excellence of the entire submarine fleet.

It was an expensive and embarrassing lesson, but one I have not forgotten.

THE SOUND OF SILENCE

Our transparency issues steadily worsened. Sailors were no longer reporting errors, and the ship could not benefit from the collective intelligence that came from sharing wins and losses. We grew silent. Even Captain Fenwick began to notice the issue when our failure of communication led to a serious breach in safety protocol.

As a young sailor training in the engine room walked past a key reactor valve, he saw that it was open, and he erroneously thought it should be closed. He turned the valve to what he believed was the proper alignment. He was wrong. He neither confirmed his action with anyone nor even documented what he had done. There was no immediate danger to the reactor, since the valve was a redundancy, but a loss redundancy is a big deal in the nuclear arena.

On the midnight watch, someone saw the error and manually fixed the valve position. Again, protocol was ignored, and the second sailor didn't file an incident report. The next day, the original sailor noticed the valve was open and—as he had done before—he closed it.

The incorrectly set valve was spotted by the next watch who *finally* followed protocol and notified the captain. Due to the severity of the breach, Captain Fenwick mustered the entire engineering department into the crew's mess.

"Men, we've had a serious situation with the reactor valve. It's okay to come forward and identify yourself if you changed the valve without documentation. It is safe to speak up. Please let me know who did this."

Crickets.

In that moment, Captain Fenwick desperately needed a culture that protected transparency and vulnerability, but he hadn't done the work to cultivate one.

"Please," he said. "I need to know how this happened. We need to fix our process."

Despite the kindness in his tone, no one spoke.

Sometime after the captain dismissed us, the men who'd first noticed the incorrectly set valve finally went to see him in private. They admitted their failure to report, as well as their fear of speaking up afterward.

Everything Grooms had accomplished slowly waned. In less than two years, we'd gone from being the best-performing ship in the fleet to nearly losing our reactor keys. We were on the brink of being pulled from missions of national security and getting tied to the dock. More importantly, our poor culture had put us at risk of a catastrophic event.

The technical competence of our crew and leaders was stellar. We had the ability to perform at the top of the fleet, but our outcomes did not match our potential. We had all stopped talking—at least to the right people, in the right situations.

NO LONGER CREW

The *Asheville* headed to its new home port of Bremerton, Washington, for a year-and-a-half overhaul. My transfer off the ship was to take place immediately upon arrival. I couldn't wait to put the *Asheville* in my rearview mirror. Not only had I received word that my wife and I were expecting our first child, but I was also anxious to escape the unbearable atmosphere on board the ship. As soon as we pulled into port and the gangway was in place, I began to disembark with my gear in hand. The chief of the boat (COB) stopped me.

"NAV, liberty is not down for the crew yet."

"COB," I replied, "I am no longer crew."

I felt a weight drop from my shoulders as I walked away.

Though it was still early in my career, I had already experienced vastly different leaders, from the punishing MFB to the thoughtful and caring Admiral Grooms.

Captain Fenwick lay in the middle. He wasn't a bad person; he just had blind spots. He prioritized his mission over his people, and he lacked empathy. Fenwick didn't connect the morale of the crew to the performance of the mission. There was little chance I'd ever turn into an MFB, but I could become a Fenwick if I wasn't careful, and I didn't want that to happen. *How would I stay attuned to my blind spots? How would I go about making sure every single member of my team knew their purpose and felt valued? How would I demonstrate grace while enforcing standards? How would I show my love?* My reflections on and answers to these questions shaped my leadership style and informed who I would become.

— CHAPTER 8 —

THE STRENGTH
OF A
BROTHERHOOD

"Brotherhood is the good deed, service to others. Brotherhood is food, shelter, and raiment, yes, but it is also the word of hope, the pat on the back, the open door, the warm hearth."

—P. L. PRATTIS

Following my time on the *Asheville*, I reported to Squadron Seven as the operations officer. The new duty gave me the opportunity to witness other commands in action. This time, I had good luck and was able to serve under two excellent commodores, Glen Niederhauser and Dennis Murphy. Both equipped me with valuable skills for my leadership toolbox. My faith in the navy began to rebound. I felt reenergized and ready to begin my next assignment.

A "HOWES-TO" GUIDE

Getting to serve as the executive officer of the USS *La Jolla* (SSN 701), stationed out of Pearl Harbor, was a double bonus for me. Not only did I get to take on a new leadership role, but I also got the opportunity to learn under Commanding Officer Brian Howes, who turned out to be amazing.

My new position gave me insight into higher-level leadership and the top-down perspective necessary to oversee an entire submarine. It also allowed me to stretch my leadership muscles. I wanted to show my team that I appreciated them and saw value in their work. I wanted to impart the confidence that comes from understanding your individual purpose as it connects to the greater purpose of a mission.

One of the most potent leadership practices I've witnessed was the method Howes developed for gathering feedback. The process he termed "Crew Top Three" was simple yet ingenious at the same time.

Once per quarter, Howes mustered the crew topside and asked them to identify their three greatest concerns. He always reminded the sailors that it didn't matter how trivial their worries might be. He cared about the pebbles in their shoes and wanted the opportunity to remove them, if possible.

At times, some would bring up paint colors or menu selections. Others would share frustrations about duty schedules or too little time in port. On occasion, crew members would mention their annoyances with navy processes or codes. The topics covered a wide range. Under Howes, the crew felt free to express their pet peeves along with deep concerns. The level of trust and psychological safety the crew had with their captain was evident in those Crew Top Three sessions.

This methodology was successful because of the trust Howes built with his sailors. He listened to their worries and suggestions and then did something about them. After sifting through the feedback, Howes would report back to the crew. He thanked them for their input and discussed the changes that would be made in response. If some complaints could not be addressed in the hoped-for manner, Howes would explain why, but he never made excuses.

The crew appreciated the captain's explanation for "no" answers almost as much as the "yes" answers he was able to give. Their trust in Captain Howes grew because they knew he had good intentions and followed up with actions.

After Crew Top Three sessions, Howes would ask for my input and allow me to problem-solve alongside him. We would start by going through all the sailors' suggestions and complaints. If Howes and I noticed a common theme, that issue was given priority. Often, the solution resulted in a new and improved written policy.

One such issue regarded hour compensation for work during "stand-down." Stand-down is typically a thirty-day period of downtime following a six-month or longer deployment. This interval—during which the workload is light, with little to no maintenance on the ship—affords sailors the opportunity to take vacations and live a somewhat normal life. Many crew members who'd been obliged to work during stand-down on weekends or after 1800 (6:00 p.m.) pointed out that they were not being adequately credited for their after-hours work.

The written solution we brought back to crew members went something like this:

> *In many cases during deployment, there is not adequate time to award compensation for late hours or weekends worked in order to meet all commitments to get the ship underway. The goal remains to have no non-duty personnel work after 1800 or on weekends. When exceptions occur, we will ensure that the division chief submits a written plan for providing compensation time for those that have to work after hours. For those that have already had to work after 1800 or during stand-down since deployment, the appropriate divisions will provide and execute a plan for compensation as directed.*

This may seem like a dry, administrative matter—certainly not one of national security—but it answered a critical problem, nonetheless. Sailors work long, hard hours while at sea and, sometimes, in port. By acknowledging and compensating those extra hours, we honored their dedication.

The Crew Top Three exercise demonstrated to the team we valued them. It proved that the command had their back. It also helped us identify blind spots. This simple give-and-take activity became a cornerstone of our communication. The transparency of leaders—and the safe psychological space established in the process—enabled vulnerability, built mutual trust, and created solid relational bonds.

Despite winning the Vice Admiral James Bond Stockdale Award and leading the *La Jolla* to a Battle "E" (an annual, highly competitive award given to only the most effective submarine teams and commands in the squadron), Howes remained humble and self-aware. Though he had a good sense of humor, he was a calm, cerebral introvert. I, on the other hand, was (and still am) an extrovert—in some ways the "yin" to his "yang." I loved addressing the crew and using my high energy to keep them on their toes.

After speaking to the crew, Howes would often ask me in private, "What do you think? How did I do?"

As the two highest-ranking officers on the ship, we spent hours together each day. I became his confidant and cheerleader. With disarming humility, Howes sought my advice and perceptions on his handling of various situations. He expected an honest opinion and voiced his appreciation of my feedback.

Leaders often find themselves in an echo chamber. Howes showed me the importance of having a trusted source of constructive criticism. He often asked for input but also welcomed unsolicited advice. Extending that psychological safety to me created the greatest level of trust I've experienced in a leader-subordinate relationship. Our bond was tight, and I would not let him fail, even if that meant I had to step in and tell him uncomfortable things. I also had no doubt he would do the same for me.

My time on the *La Jolla* under Howes brought me back to a sense of family. I was beginning to see just how much positive energy I received through sacrificial service to those in my circle of influence.

Fortunately, Howes's replacement, Pete Hildreth, continued to nurture culture and create a cohesive team. His arrival didn't take the wind out of our sails; it only strengthened it.

A BROTHERHOOD LIKE NO OTHER

When a portion of another elite group, SEAL Delivery Vehicle Team One (SDV1), deployed with the *La Jolla* crew, their overwhelmingly tight bonds reinforced the importance of a work family.

The *La Jolla* was equipped with a SEAL Delivery Vehicle (SDV) dry dock shelter. An SDV is the type of tiny submarine you might see in a James Bond movie. Our dry dock shelter enabled the SDV to attach to our ship, allowing the Navy SEALs to enter and exit directly from our submerged submarine. *La Jolla* was tasked to deploy to the western Pacific, deliver the SEALs to their highly classified mission, and then await their return.

SDV1 were as boisterous as they were tight-knit, and their presence on board infused a sense of energy. I found them fascinating.

When one of them stood next to me in the control room prior to getting underway, I noticed he had a patch with the letters NDN on the shoulder of his uniform. I wondered what the letters meant and assumed they formed an acronym for something related to the Gulf War. Curiosity got the better of me, and I finally asked. The SEAL explained that the letters stood for "Indian," the heritage of his good friend and fellow SEAL who had been killed. I then noticed several of them had the same memorial patch. Impressed with their strong bond, I never imagined submariners honoring a shipmate in a similar way. The SEALs were indeed a brotherhood.

As we were preparing for the SEALs' mission, word came that SEAL Team One had suffered a substantial loss. Part of their team had been on a covert mission in Afghanistan and come under heavy gunfire. Only one SEAL, Marcus Luttrell, survived the ordeal.

In his book *Lone Survivor*, Luttrell gives a firsthand account of the attack and the unbelievable sacrifice of Navy SEAL Michael Murphy and others on the team. A Hollywood movie of the same name also memorializes the tragic story.

But at the time it happened, no one on *La Jolla* knew the real significance of the event. The SEALs on board were profoundly saddened by the news, but they remained stoic and carried on. They pushed aside their pain to serve a higher calling.

VALUING TRUST

The SEALs' work-family bonds were stronger than any I'd ever witnessed. Their culture was extraordinary.

Author and speaker Simon Sinek spent time with the SEALs and learned that the critical factor in their success is trust. An old military saying they shared gets to the root of trustworthiness: "I trust you with my life, but do I trust you with my money and my wife?"[12]

When Sinek asked the SEALs how they went about choosing who would serve in their most elite teams, they drew a chart. The Y-axis was labeled "Performance" and represented skills on the battlefield, while the X-axis was labeled "Trust" and represented performance in life.

Obviously, they had little regard for low performers with low trust. Equally obvious was the appeal of a teammate with high marks in both performance and trust. What was surprising, though, was how the SEALs evaluated candidates in the remaining two quadrants. Sinek describes it this way: "What they learned is that this person, the high performer of low trust, is a toxic leader and a toxic team member. And they would rather have a medium performer of high trust, sometimes even a low performer of high trust . . . over [the high performer of low trust]. This is the highest performing organization on the planet, and [the low performer of high trust] is more important than [the high performer of low trust], and the problem in business is that we have lopsided metrics."[13]

Trust is not just developed at a team level. Through shared experiences, individual members of a SEAL team develop one-on-one relationships with each other. These personal relationships are especially critical to SEAL leaders who must take their men to the very edge. When a SEAL is told to do something that seems physically or psychologically impossible, trusting that what the leader says is possible *is* indeed possible will help the SEAL push further. As much as they train, plan, and gather intelligence, SEALs cannot foresee every variable. Sometimes, a SEAL must go into a hellhole. And if his leader says it's necessary, he will do it—if he has confidence in his leader.

AFTER ACTION

After a mission, military teams will run back through the mission, discussing their successes and failures and documenting them in an after-action report. Team members are encouraged to speak up and discuss what could have been done better. Daniel Coyle interviewed Navy SEAL Dave Cooper about these debriefings for his book *The Culture Code*:

> "It's got to be safe to talk," Cooper says. "Rank switched off, humility switched on. You're looking for that moment where people can say, 'I screwed that up.' In fact, I'd say those might be the most important four words any leader can say: '*I screwed that up.*'"[14]

That type of vulnerability and accountability reveals truth, and truth is one of the most valuable ingredients of trust.

My interactions with the SEALS on *La Jolla* still inspire me. They made me even more certain that building a familial bond is vital to achieving a legendary culture, and that a team must have psychological safety to reach its highest potential.

My clear takeaway: *every* leader should wake up in the morning on a mission to advance trust.

—CHAPTER 9—

FINDING A PURPOSE

"Make your work to be in keeping with your purpose."

—Leonardo da Vinci

The time a submariner serves as an executive officer is short—on average, only eighteen months. It was soon time to move on to my next assignment. So far, I had spent a significant part of my career in the navy at sea. As an XO, I was rarely home, and when I was, I wasn't entirely present.

I was gone so often that my departures became traumatic. If my three-year-old daughter heard my keys jingle when I was home, she'd come running to me and hang on with all her might. To leave the house without a scene, I had to sneak out.

One incident was particularly jarring. I had just returned home from an extended underway and was headed out again for another two months. In my haste, I forgot to keep my keys silent. My daughter rushed in and grabbed onto me with no intention of letting go. I had to peel her off and hand her to my wife. Both of my girls had tear-filled eyes.

I wondered, *What am I doing? Is this worth it?*

My wife and children sacrificed a lot for my career and my service. They needed me home every night for a change.

AN UNEXPECTED OPPORTUNITY

I thought about my choices. One would presume that shore duty would allow me to be home each night. However, many shore tours required a lot of travel or short underways to support submarine operations. A tour at the Pentagon would also mean hellishly long days and an exhausting commute in Washington, DC, traffic.

I knew unequivocally that I wanted to spend more time at home, and I didn't want to risk working for another MFB or Captain Fenwick, but service members can't dictate their next duty station. I could give my preferences, but I knew the needs of the navy would be the detailer's priority.

The navy screened me for command on my first look, which gave me good options. I contacted my detailer, Jim Waters, a compassionate leader who knew firsthand about family sacrifice. I had confidence in him to help me.

"Bob, tell me what you want. I'll do whatever I can to make it work," he said.

"Jim, look, whatever you do, don't send me to Washington, DC. I don't want to work incredibly long hours for top brass at the Pentagon. I need a break."

His reply gave me hope: "You got it, Bob. I won't send you to DC."

He called me back a few days later with several options. One in Colorado Springs, Colorado, held the potential for a great deal of family time. However, nothing in detailing is ever a sure thing.

Several months later, while home christening my son, I received a call with a 901 area code. I knew it was Jim.

"Jim, don't send me to DC," I answered without preamble. "If you say anything about going to DC to work as an aide for some admiral, I'm gonna—"

"Wait, wait," Jim interrupted, "This is the opportunity of a lifetime."

I listened but was leery.

"The submarine force wants to nominate you as the naval aide to the president of the United States," Jim continued.

I certainly wasn't expecting that! The possibility wasn't even on my radar.

The White House assignment would require the highest security clearance, Yankee White. I'd also have to travel with the president to many of his destinations—domestic and foreign. Trips to Topeka or Los Angeles were one thing, but they didn't compare in complexity to trips to the Middle East or Africa. Many times, the president's military aide (MILAIDE) is the only one in uniform near the president and is heavily scrutinized by foreign dignitaries. To help the president accomplish his missions, I'd need a steely-eyed demeanor coupled with a courteous attitude.

Additionally, I'd be responsible for carrying the black briefcase—affectionately called the nuclear football—that contains the nuclear launch codes.

The football's history dates back to just after the Cuban Missile Crisis, when the government recognized the need for nuclear decision-making and control to be mobile and accessible to the president at all times. The technology of the football has advanced over the years, but its core function has remained the same.

The president must be prepared to launch a retaliatory nuclear strike at any time to counter a threat from another nuclear-capable country. Deterrence through mutual assured destruction prevents loss of life. World War I and World War II caused nearly 100 million deaths.[15] Deaths from the Cold War to the present total less than 10 percent of that number.[16] The simple explanation for this dramatic reduction is that the threat of nuclear retaliation discourages conflict.

The launch system is protected by multiple redundancies and verification requirements from the president, MILAIDE, and other service members at the launch site. Should the original fall into the wrong hands, the codes held by the president would be changed and power shifted to another football. The vice president has a football as well. If the president is incapacitated, even by a simple medical procedure like a colonoscopy, authority to authorize the launch of nuclear missiles formally transfers to the vice president.

While Secret Service agents provide the president micro-level protection, the five military aides (one from each branch of service) offer a macro response to threats, such as support for exfiltration. MILAIDES have tactical control over all military assets that safeguard the president. They share responsibilities and take turns serving in the capacity of emergency actions (EA) officer, White House operations officer, ceremonial aide, executive assistant, and personal aide. Through intelligence gathering, communications, and employment of assets, military aides make sure the president can perform his role as commander in chief from air, land, or sea. This effort involves hundreds of personnel as well as coordination with the Secret Service, Marine One, Air Force One, the Department of Defense, and the White House.

So, it's a big job.

Although I told my detailer I didn't want an assignment or anything to do with the whole DC political machine, he encouraged me to go anyway.

"You probably won't get it," Jim said. "Six or seven other guys are interviewing for the position. Just go to the White House, do the interview, check out the cherry blossoms, and enjoy a few days in DC."

Detailers can be great salespeople.

Dan Bongino began his time on the Secret Service Presidential Protection Detail in 2006 and writes about his experience in *Life inside the Bubble: Why a Top-Ranked Secret Service Agent Walked Away from It All*. Long hours, specific attire based on location, a constant state of readiness, and even a lack of freedom to go to the bathroom are all part of the job for those brave agents. I assumed life as a military aide would mirror those conditions to some degree. Yet, a part of me felt it was too incredible of an opportunity to waste.

I talked it over with Stephanie. Although she had her heart set on Colorado, we both concluded that the navy was presenting me with the chance of a lifetime. I needed to try for it. Jim took the pressure off by downplaying my likelihood of getting the job, so Stephanie and I both assumed the opportunity would end with the interview.

NOTHING TO HIDE

With that, I headed for Washington, DC. The current military aides would conduct the interviews because they knew the job and president's expectations better than anyone. I figured they'd ask the typical questions: Why do you think you'd make a good aide to the president? What is your experience? What was your greatest challenge?

With nothing to lose, I planned to go in relaxed, just be myself, and not overthink it. Nonchalance at its finest.

I spent the first day working on the background and security check. I knew the rigorous security clearance would thin the herd of nominees quickly. Inside the New Executive Office Building (NEOB) across the street from the White House, I sat in a small room with sparse furnishings, a telephone, and the lead investigator—hardly a red-carpet reception.

The investigator tossed a book of questions on the table for me to complete. It felt like a scene in a spy movie. The only thing missing was a single bulb hanging over the interrogation table.

"Call me when you're done," he said matter-of-factly.

I opened the booklet to find dozens and dozens of questions—some highlighted, some not. The highlights were random, with no particular pattern. "Have you ever had a speeding ticket?" was highlighted, but "Have you ever sold secrets to a foreign national?" was not. Perplexed, I finished the book, called the number, and waited.

When the investigator returned, he started digging into the highlighted questions. I began to realize those were the questions someone might lie on, especially someone who already had high-security clearance.

Although I had nothing to hide, the investigator made me uncomfortable. I felt sweat rolling down my back, beneath my service dress blues. I wondered if the room was kept hot intentionally.

The investigator scanned the questions and then looked up with skepticism. "You've never gotten a speeding ticket?"

I smiled and leaned forward. "No, I have never gotten a speeding ticket ... but I didn't say I never got pulled over."

That disarmed him, and he laughed. Then, I told him about the time I ran over my friend.

It wasn't as bad as it sounds, but I felt compelled to explain.

"On a trip from New York to the 'Head of the Occoquan' regatta in Virginia, I was driving a van full of my college crew teammates while our coach pulled the trailer with the boats. Several guys needed to relieve themselves, but we were in a time crunch, and I had no way to tell the coach we needed to stop.

"As we approached the I-95 tolls right before Virginia, one of my teammates said, 'Go to the far-right booth. There's a huge line. The guys can run into the woods and get back before we take off.'

"The toll line went faster than expected, and the bathroom break took too long. I drove through the toll as they reached the van. I was in a hurry, so I kept rolling forward as they began to jump in.

"Someone yelled, 'All in!' so I hit the gas.

"We heard a thump, and I assumed we hit a speed bump. Then, my buddy Vic Sammons yelled, 'Holy shit! You just ran over Poliwada!'

"Apparently, Ken Poliwada—who was now screaming in pain—hadn't been all the way in when I took off and I'd run over his right leg with the rear tire. We ended up in the emergency room. Amazingly, he only had some nasty bruising—no broken bones. He made a full recovery in about a week.

"Of course, I felt terrible for hurting Ken. But I also regretted that the coach had trusted me to drive the van and I had let him down.

"The responding police officer told me he was going to issue me a ticket, but he must never have turned it in."

When I was finished, I had no idea how the interview had gone. I hoped my story had shown that I wasn't hiding any skeletons.

FROM DOUBT TO ASSURANCE

On day two, an army sergeant picked me up from my hotel for the drive to the White House. I later learned the interviewing MILAIDEs asked these drivers whether candidates sat in the front or back, if we talked with them, and what we discussed. In other words, every encounter we had was being evaluated. Unaware of this at the time, I asked the driver if I could sit in the front with him and had a friendly chat as we drove.

I was escorted to the East Room of the White House, where I stood in awe of the grandiose decor. A six-foot-four pilot who had been nominated from another branch of the navy was also there to interview for the position. Though I kept in shape and continued to run marathons, I didn't have his stature or movie-star looks. Self-doubt started to creep in. In my head, I was still the fat little farm boy from Dunkirk. Beginning to feel like an imposter, I expected someone to tap me on the shoulder at any moment and say, "Hey, buddy, what are you doing here? There's been a mistake. Go home."

I kept trying to tell myself just to enjoy the experience. I wouldn't get the job. I should simply appreciate the honor and the opportunity.

I was led past tourists and into areas of the White House the public never sees. Stepping through a vaulted door and into a basement, I entered the Presidential Emergency Operations Center—the same room the president returned to after the 9/11 attacks. There, I faced all the current military aides, with representatives from the army, navy, coast guard, marines, and air force. They asked me the standard strengths-and-weaknesses questions, as well as others that surprised me: "What if you don't get this job?" "What is your most embarrassing moment?"

They seemed to be assessing my motives and trustworthiness.

I tried to promote my qualifications without overselling. I also reminded myself that I had an excellent assignment waiting. I told the MILAIDEs that I'd be fine if I didn't get the job—and that it was an honor to be interviewed among so many highly qualified candidates.

When I made it back to my hotel, I looked at flight options to return to Hawaii early. I didn't even entertain the thought I'd be selected.

That evening, Keith Davids, the current navy MILAIDE called. I figured he'd tell me, "Thanks for coming, and good luck in the future." What he actually said was entirely unexpected.

"We'd like you to come back for another round of interviews. You and one other candidate will meet with Admiral Mark Fox, the director of the White House Military Office, and Joe Hagin, deputy chief of staff for operations."

I was so taken aback that I said, "Keith, this is Bob Roncska. Just to confirm, you called the right number?" I probably stuttered too.

Well, he *had* called the correct number, and I had, in fact, made the cut.

Less than twenty-four hours later, Joe Hagin shook my hand and said, "Congratulations, you are the next naval aide to the president of the United States."

Again, I was stunned.

Keith Davids congratulated me afterward and said, "This is going to change your life." And it did.

The tremendous responsibility of carrying the codes for the president, and the opportunity to work directly with one of the most outstanding leaders this nation has ever had, George W. Bush, was priceless.

Shortly after my assignment was finalized, Admiral Fox sent Stephanie a letter. It had been typed and addressed to "Mrs. Roncska." The admiral had crossed out the formal name, changed it to "Stephanie," and added a handwritten note: "We look forward to your becoming part of the White House military office family."

The kind gesture showed he cared enough to know his team and learn the names of their spouses. It eased Stephanie's transition and stood in stark contrast to the lack of respect the commands of the *West Virginia* and *Asheville* had shown her. Thoughtful acts don't need to require a lot of effort or time, but they can go a long way toward making others feel valued.

I didn't know it then, but I was about to learn many more lessons on leading with love that would help me evolve as a leader and serve me in profound ways.

PART THREE: Leading with Love at the Highest Levels

— CHAPTER 10 —

A Sense
of
Belonging

"People don't care how much you know until they know how much you care. By establishing a relationship first, you qualify yourself to speak truth into their lives, even when it may hurt."

—John C. Maxwell

Our family settled in the DC suburb of Arlington, Virginia—a significant change for us. My daughter had only known the balmy weather of Hawaii and preferred life in shorts and flip-flops (or "slippahs," as we had come to call them).

Colder weather aside, I welcomed the new routine and the opportunity to be home every night during my training period. Of course, there was nothing "routine" about working in the White House. My desk was in the Military Aides' Office in the East Wing, and my security clearance gave me access to much of the West Wing. The mission-critical work—laced with a little bit of intrigue—thrilled me. On a scale from one to ten, the urge to "pinch myself to see if I was dreaming" was an eleven.

I wasn't particularly political, so my initial excitement about my presidential detail came from working for the office versus the man himself. In time, I would observe firsthand the character and leadership style of our forty-third president and find that the lessons he taught me were my greatest takeaway from my duty as a military aide.

WAR ON TERROR

Just eight months after George W. Bush was sworn into office, the horrific events of September 11, 2001, took place. Thousands upon thousands of young men and women answered the call to serve their country. Some sought revenge, others sought justice, and some simply wanted to do their part. On the evening of the attack, President Bush addressed the nation with anger, determination, and resolve:

> *The search is underway for those who are behind these evil acts. I've directed the full resources of our intelligence and law enforcement communities to find those responsible and to bring them to justice. We will make no distinction between the terrorists who committed these acts and those who harbor them.*[17]

Those of us already serving immediately readied for war. Within one month, the military had boots on the ground in Afghanistan, where intelligence showed the Taliban harbored the terrorists who'd attacked America. Two years later, coalition forces invaded Iraq, seeking to overthrow the tyrannical rule of Saddam Hussein, search for weapons of mass destruction, and bring stability to the Middle East. The two-front "War on Terror" would rage for years. All the while, President Bush's administration continued its agenda to improve the nation's infrastructure, grow the economy, and push funding for HIV/AIDS testing and medication.

My role at the White House began in August 2006, five years into the conflict. Earlier that year, President Bush had delivered the State of the Union address to a nation tiring of war. He ended his remarks with a call to action:

> *Fellow citizens, we've been called to leadership in a period of consequence. We've entered a great ideological conflict we did nothing to invite. We see great changes in science and commerce that will influence all our lives. Sometimes it can seem that history is turning in a wide arc toward an unknown shore. Yet the destination of history is determined by human action, and every great movement of history comes to a point of choosing.*[18]

He left the nation's listeners with a final question: "Will we turn back or finish well?"[19]

OPEN TO ADVICE

The outgoing naval MILAIDE, Keith Davids, oversaw my training and taught me the basics of the role in his final two months. Keith was the epitome of a SEAL. Everyone loved and respected him, and I quickly realized I had big shoes to fill.

I'd seen President Bush walk by with staffers and been in a room with him for various duties, but I didn't formally meet him until Keith earned his departure medal and coveted, authentic NFL football. (Signed by the president and other military aides, the traditional MILAIDE gift is a memento of time spent carrying the nuclear "football.")

I had my first genuine interaction with President Bush at a tribute to the recently deceased former President Gerald Ford in Grand Rapids, Michigan. Most events are highly orchestrated, but planned movements are kept confidential as a matter of security.

Initially, the trip didn't require me to do anything with the president. But at the very last minute before President Bush's arrival, Jason Recher, special assistant to the president, asked me to hand Bush a bouquet of flowers for him to lay by the curved stone wall of President Ford's tomb.

I realize it sounds awfully simple. As a nuclear submarine officer, I'd operated billion-dollar equipment and handled some pretty sticky situations. But this was the president of the United States—surrounded by the national press!

No protocol existed for laying flowers at the tomb. I didn't like the last-minute change and panicked slightly over the uncertainty. As sweat began to roll, multiple questions filled my mind: *Where do I stand? What is the sequence? What exactly do I do?*

Jason reiterated, "All you need to do is hand him the flowers. Don't worry."

I stood halfway up the walk to the burial site, staring straight ahead and holding the eighteen wrapped roses at arm's length, like a sailor extending his weapon. Everyone remained silent during the somber moment. Seeing the president approach in my peripheral vision, I heard a cacophony of camera shutters.

I handed him the white flowers and thought my task finished, until President Bush asked in a hushed tone, "Should I stand them up or just lay them down?"

He was asking me, a military aide, where to lay a bouquet of flowers. It may seem trivial, but it indicated the president's respect for the military's opinion on things great and small. Every move a president makes comes under heavy scrutiny. President Bush had to be able to trust his staff to deliver sound advice.

My adrenaline went into hyperdrive as my fear of messing up soared. I didn't want to let my new boss down, so I simply made the call.

"Mr. President, I'm going to walk with you, and then you just stand them up next to his name." President Bush took my advice, and the event flowed perfectly.

He hardly knew me, yet he asked for my opinion and followed my lead. The small gesture of trust created within me a sense of belonging. It reignited that old feeling Grooms had inspired many years ago. I didn't take the trust the president placed in me for granted, and I prepared to serve him without reserve.

CREATING A SENSE OF BELONGING

Over time, I learned that the president—clearly and confidently in charge—had no issue with receiving input from those around him. In his memoir *Courage and Consequence*, Karl Rove, senior advisor to President Bush, writes about the direct access the president granted to all of his senior staff. In essence, Bush created a team of equals. This collaborative body had the freedom to interject and debate the issues at hand with full psychological safety. The president might challenge someone on their convictions, but he would also accept "I don't know" as an answer. He just wanted to make sure his people gave him their honest opinions. "If you demonstrated you could operate this way, you won Bush's trust. And with that trust came his loyalty; he understood it ran both ways."[20]

Along with the high-stakes tasks that were part of our daily duties, President Bush included his team in the everyday aspects of life, creating within us a sense of belonging. He often asked us to join him for bike rides at places like Beltsville or Fort Belvoir, a military base near Washington, DC, dubbing our small group "Peloton One." Biking through the woods was a particularly favorite pastime for the president. The more complex and technical the course, the better.

President Bush had a competitive streak. I had to bring my "A" game on those bike rides. I was fit, but no matter how hard I pushed, he pushed harder. He managed to outmaneuver us all and speed through the courses. The friendly competition and opportunity to play hard together bonded us and added to our sense of belonging.

To make rides more interesting, the president invited occasional guests to join Peloton One. NFL coach and former quarterback Jim Zorn was one such guest. Though athletic, Coach Zorn's prowess did not extend to mountain biking. He wanted to prepare for the bike ride, so I arranged an opportunity for him to practice on our Fort Belvoir course beforehand. Still, on the day of the ride, Coach Zorn couldn't keep up. I hung back with him to help him get his bike up hills and to redirect him to dirt service trails on the outskirts of the course, giving him a chance to catch his breath.

At the end of the day's ride and out of earshot of Zorn, President Bush asked, "How'd he do?"

I smiled and said, "Sir, you smoked him!"

He chuckled and, while looking back at the coach, said wryly, "Welcome to the NFL!"

CARVING A PATH

Activity was an important stress release for the president. During more difficult times, such as the surge in Iraq, he would blow off steam with physical labor at Crawford Ranch, his home in Texas. Riding challenging new bike trails helped him too. These pursuits didn't pull the president away from his job. He always rose early and worked incredibly hard, even when he was at Camp David or the ranch for a respite. The exertion simply cleared his head and offered a much-needed outlet.

Riding the same bike paths can become monotonous. For security reasons, the president could not go to just any trail. He enjoyed the ones at Camp David, but we needed something closer to the White House. I took it upon myself to find a challenging course or build one if necessary. I discovered a great spot to build a trail at Fort Belvoir. I ran my idea by the head of the Secret Service, but he shot it down due to security concerns. Pushing back, I insisted we could design the course in such a way as to keep the president in their sights the entire ride.

My persistence paid off. Two months later, Peloton One enjoyed its inaugural ride on the new trail. The look on the president's face as he entered the course made me so happy. I was proud my efforts relieved his stress in some small way.

Creating difficult routes and carving out new bike trails became a passion for me. The first course helped me earn the confidence of the Secret Service. They saw that my plans considered the safety of the president and their ability to protect him. That trust led to their approval of more trails, including ones at Crawford Ranch.

At the risk of sounding corny, creating bike courses for the president became an expression of my gratitude and love. It was the type of thing I'd do for a member of my family, and it grew from the sense of belonging I felt.

NAVY BOB

Nicknames can express familiarity, camaraderie, or simply be a way to differentiate one person from another. My nickname served that last purpose at first; it grew to mean much more.

Beltsville, Maryland, where the Secret Service trains, had good trails, but they got too muddy after a rain. When I was still new to the team, a group of us installed some mini, six-foot bridges over the worst spots to overcome that problem.

On the way back to the White House after a ride with the new bridges, the president asked his personal aide, Jared Weinstein, "Who put in those little bridges?"

Jared listed off our names, but when he said my name, the president stopped him, "Bob who?"

"You know," Jared said, "Navy Bob."

The name grew legs. From then on, I was known to President Bush and everyone in the White House as "Navy Bob." Jared later joked that coming up with my nickname was one of his greatest accomplishments. The moniker made me feel like I'd been initiated into a club, and I was one of the gang. I continue to answer proudly to Navy Bob.

COLLISION COURSE

Few things are more bonding than shared experiences—especially calamities. During the Beijing Olympics, the president was given the opportunity to ride the mountain bike trails built for the event. A core group of riders, including me, other off-duty MILAIDES, and advance staff, were lucky enough to ride along with him.

As one would expect, the course was extremely challenging, loaded with steep inclines and boulders. The president was in great shape and a technically sound biker, but he wasn't an Olympian. For his safety, he avoided the dangerous sections of the trail.

As we approached one double black diamond, President Bush wisely dismounted, picked up his bike, and walked to the bottom of the hill. The next several riders followed suit. But then, my fearless marine counterpart, Mark "Ziggy" Thompson, stayed on his bike and headed straight down the trail.

I approached the edge and peered over. The other riders looked up at me, smiling and egging me on: "Come on, Navy Bob! You can do it! Mark did!"

It looked like a sheer, thirty-foot drop, riddled with rocks and other hazards. But one of my most significant weaknesses is my inability to back down from a challenge. I couldn't let my MILAIDE brother—a marine—outdo me.

As I started my descent, I realized my shoe wasn't clipped into my bike. Instead of continuing with my foot unattached to the pedal, I glanced down and attempted to reattach my shoe. When I looked up, I found myself on a collision course with a giant rock and no time to take corrective action. The bike and boulder collided, launching me into the air. The steepness of the hill intensified my fall, and I plummeted eight feet before my chin and right leg crashed against two separate rocks. Voices around me echoed with "ohs!" and "ows!" and "oh my Gods!"

In shock and unaware of my injuries, I recovered my bike and rode the short distance to the finish line. I thought my worst injury was to my pride, but as it turned out, my chin was busted enough to require stitches. Before the medical team could perform their duties, I posed with them and President Bush for pictures and received a few pats on the back. After that, Dr. Jeffrey Kuhlman and Cindy Wright, the president's physician and nurse, whisked me away and attended to my injuries.

From left to right: President George W. Bush, Robert Roncska, Joe Passanante, and Cindy Wright

SMALL MOMENTS OF GREAT IMPACT

My wife met the president for the first time at the Christmas party given for the military who served at the White House and other DC area senior brass. President Bush had a quick wit and chatted easily with the many people he met every day. Still, as she was preparing for the event, Stephanie felt nervous and unsure of what to expect. I briefed her on that weekend's bike ride, guessing that it would be the subject the president chose to talk about. As it turned out, I guessed wrong.

Following their introduction at the party, President Bush looked at Stephanie and with all seriousness asked, "Do you call him Navy Bob at home, too?"

A mischievous grin and a chuckle answered Stephanie's response: "Only when I am mad at him." I appreciated the president's efforts to ease my wife's tension and include her in the fun.

In the military, we are always celebrating promotions, end-of-tours, or new honors with various ceremonies. About midway through my time in the White House, the navy promoted me from Lieutenant-Commander to Commander. As the president did with all the MILAIDEs, he took time out of his extraordinarily busy schedule to celebrate my promotion in the Oval Office, making sure to include my family and select friends as well. He pinned my new rank on one shoulder while Stephanie pinned the other. It was neither something President Bush *had* to do nor a pivotal life moment for him personally. But having the commander in chief recognize my accomplishments was an experience of a lifetime for *me*.

From left to right: President George W. Bush, Cmdr. Robert Roncska, and Stephanie Roncska

The same sense of belonging the president created within his team and extended to our families was also fostered by the First Lady in so many magical ways.

One time, Laura Bush invited the staff's children to watch *Horton Hears a Who* at the White House theater. Another time, at Camp David, the on-duty staff's families were welcomed to the mess hall for Christmas dinner and a meet and greet with the president and Mrs. Bush.

The year I had Christmas duty at Camp David, my daughter, Sophia, was five, and my son, Zack, was two. As cute and chubby toddlers do, Zack was stealing the show. Mrs. Bush, a teacher and mother with great intuition, noticed that my daughter was not receiving as much attention. The First Lady got down to Sophia's level and made a specific effort to engage her in conversation.

Stephanie and I already admired Mrs. Bush for her worldwide humanitarian efforts and championing of education and women's rights. But seeing the First Lady take the time to make our daughter feel special spoke volumes to us about her kind and generous spirit. These small moments often have the greatest impact.

A CARING MINDSET

It's easy to imagine that anyone would have a good time working at the White House. But friends of mine who have worked for other administrations have told me they didn't feel the same sort of magic. The love the Bushes demonstrated for those who worked with them was always evident. They trusted me as an expert, showing their respect and thoughtfulness, and they always considered and appreciated my family, as well, making sure to include them in activities.

One of my favorite things about the Bush administration was the feeling of fun and camaraderie that prevailed, fueled by President Bush's self-deprecating sense of humor. He leaned into his reputation for getting tongue tied, for example, and kept a plaque that read "strategery" on his desk at Camp David.

The Bush family genuinely cared for people and used their influence to serve in so many ways. I was blessed to witness many of their acts of compassion, their heartfelt conversations, and the emotions that accompanied each expression of empathy. The president took his role as commander in chief seriously and demonstrated an especially high level of concern for those serving under his command.

The culture the Bushes created with love inspired me to do more. I wanted to positively impact others in the same way. I believed the magic wasn't exclusive to working in the White House and that it could be replicated anywhere if the environment was right. I wished to honor them by paying it forward and creating that nurturing environment. I wanted that same magic for all the teams I had the opportunity to lead.

— CHAPTER 11 —

The Need for Compassion

"Use power to help people. For we are given power not to advance our own purpose nor to make a great show in the world, nor a name. There is but one just use of power, and it is to serve people."

—George W. Bush

The weeks I spent on duty at Crawford Ranch stand out in my time as a MILAIDE. The war in Iraq was surging. Every morning, I'd receive a casualty report and one-page summary of world events from the situation room at 5:00 a.m. Then I'd drive the short distance from my quarters to the Secret Service outpost near the president's front door and wait to deliver my report.

A thousand stars lit the sky. The predawn quiet of the remote spot filled me with a kind of peace, despite the sobering daily news. The Secret Service agents and I would exchange whispered greetings while we waited for the president to wake. At 5:30 on the dot, the breezeway light would come on. A creature of habit, the president would start the coffee pot, attend to morning necessities, and then step out of his house. That was my cue.

NO CAMERAS WATCHING

President Bush would always greet me with a nod and say, "Navy Bob, how are you doing this morning?"

"Good morning, Mr. President. I'm good."

"How did we do last night?" Our troops were always first on his mind.

On good days, I would tell him, "Mr. President, we did not lose anyone."

When there were no casualties, President Bush couldn't control his exuberance. His voice would get excited, and he'd start chatting about the day ahead. "All right! Are we going to work on that bike trail next to the creek later, or should we cut some trees before our ride?"

I'd finish the synopsis of world events and hand over the documents senior staff had sent.

As he accepted the paperwork, he'd look me in the eyes and thank me.

I could feel his relief. I relished those days myself, knowing that no family would have to hear that unwanted knock at the door.

On the days when we suffered casualties, my stomach churned. I felt anguish thinking of the pain suffered by the service members' families, and I dreaded sharing that anguish with President Bush.

"Mr. President, I'm sorry to report we lost four service members."

His countenance would immediately change. He'd take the briefing from me with a simple "thank you," and then walk back inside his house.

No banter. No plans for the day. Just deeply felt grief.

I learned a great deal about leadership at those predawn meetings. There were no cameras or reporters around to see the president's concern. It was only me in those moments watching him bear the heavy outcome of challenging choices he'd had to make. His humility shone through, and he displayed one of the best examples of servant leadership I've ever witnessed.

I'll never forget the day I sat with the president on Air Force One waiting to deplane and head into a nearby conference center.

A staff member stepped in and said, "Mr. President, there's a last-minute thing that came up. We have a wounded warrior outside, and he'd love to meet you. Just be warned, he doesn't have any legs, he's missing an arm, and has this huge indentation in his head. Would you be willing to meet with him?"

"Absolutely!" the president answered.

There was no press, but the usual line of dignitaries—governors, senators, and the like—

waited near the bottom of the steps to meet the president. I watched him descend the steps, pass the VIPs, and head straight for the service member who waited under the wing in his wheelchair. President Bush jogged over to the wounded warrior for a big hug. They both had smiles of joy on their faces as they chatted for over five minutes. It was just one of the many off-camera interactions I witnessed that showed how deeply and authentically the president cared about those who served under him.

President George W. Bush and Robert Roncska at Crawford Ranch

A WISH TO HONOR

Tony Snow began serving as the White House press secretary in May of 2006. He was a close friend of the president and a highly valued member of the executive staff. Unfortunately, Snow was battling colon cancer and because of his illness, ultimately decided to resign his position in September 2007.

I accompanied the president and Snow for the press secretary's final ride in Marine One—a short trip from Quantico to the White House. Also on board the helicopter were Joe Hagin, deputy chief of operations, and Joe Clancy, deputy special agent in charge.

With the nuclear football tucked neatly between my feet, I sat on a bench seat near the president, listening through secure channels to the constant communication of the support team through my headset. As we approached DC, Joe Clancy and I received the typical situation report (SITREP) from the on-site Secret Service agent. The SITREP usually gave the number of guests and members of the press and other necessary details (like confirmation that the family dogs were inside). This time, the report also made us aware there was a Gold Star Family—a family of a fallen soldier—waiting to meet the president in the Diplomatic Reception Room. This was a highly unusual spot for the family to be asked to wait, and I knew it would present the president with a quandary.

Typically, when a president returns to the White House in Marine One, he walks alone across the lawn, past spectators and ever-present cameras, to the Oval Office. On occasion, heads of state are given the privilege of making this walk beside the president and in front of the crowd. Wishing to honor his press secretary, President Bush had asked Snow ahead of time if he'd make the walk across the lawn with him. The president mentioned the plan several times, clearly excited to demonstrate his respect for Snow in this way.

Gold Star Families were also a top priority for President Bush. He recognized their sacrifice and made every effort to welcome the many such families that visited the White House. When I learned there was a family waiting to meet him in the Diplomatic Reception Room, I knew President Bush would be torn over which direction to head.

If the president didn't already know about the Gold Star Family, I thought it would be easier for him if he learned of their presence after his walk with Snow. First, though, I needed to ascertain whether the president knew or not. I communicated with Clancy, then with Hagin, and finally, via the pilot, with Jared Weinstein, the president's personal aide. The rotors of the helicopter slowed to a stop before I received confirmation one way or the other.

To my frustration, Hagin spoke to the president as soon as it was quiet enough to be openly heard.

"Mr. President, there is a Gold Star Family in the Dip Room."

Taken off guard, the president became visibly troubled by the choice he'd now have to make—honor his friend with the planned distinction or head a different way to meet the family.

Knowing how much President Bush cared for both parties and sharing that love and respect for them, I made the quick decision to solve the president's dilemma by greeting the visitors myself and bringing them to him.

"Mr. President, you can still walk Mr. Snow across the lawn," I said.

He relaxed a little and looked at me expectantly.

"The family was able to watch your landing, and when you're done with Mr. Snow, we'll have them escorted into the Oval. I'm sure they will be excited to meet you there."

Pleased with that answer, President Bush turned for his last walk with Tony Snow.

The love and respect the president regularly demonstrated toward others cultivated loyalty and yielded admiration in those who served under him. Like I did in this instance, the president's team sought out ways to make his life easier and demonstrate our love in return.

CHAMPIONS OF GOOD

There's a tendency for pundits and historians to critique a president and his administration through a political lens. If they don't like a president's conservative—or liberal—approach, detractors will find nothing but fault with the man himself.

As I said before, I'm not particularly political. I have no desire to debate the merits of President Bush's domestic and foreign policies. I will defend his character, though. Sitting as closely to him as I did, I know for certain that his decisions were driven by compassion and a desire to do the best he could for the American people.

His concern for others extended beyond our borders, as he championed humanitarian efforts around the world. The First Lady also took an active role in foreign matters with goodwill visits to Africa and trips to Afghanistan.

Mrs. Bush championed the causes of women and education in Afghanistan and backed her support with pledges of financial resources. One can imagine the powerful impact her presence and authority made in a country that prevented girls from entering most schools.

Despite the power and prestige that accompanied their roles, President and Mrs. Bush never demonstrated arrogance or elitism. They led humbly, listened to the wisdom of advisors, and worked for the good of their country in the ways they thought best.

The strength of character I saw in them meant so much more to me than their political leanings. They were people who cared about me, people I could trust. They lived according to the principle that President George H. W. Bush had spoken about at his own inaugural address: "There is but one use of power, and it is to serve people."[21]

― CHAPTER 12 ―

BUILT ON TRUST

"The best proof of love is trust."

—JOYCE BROTHERS

One of the greatest leadership assets is the ability to give and receive trust. Trust forms the foundation of a strong culture. I don't need to wax eloquent on the subject because many great thinkers have already done the topic justice. However, I can speak to my experience serving under a president skilled in building trust as well as my own efforts as a leader.

Some might consider trust building a "soft" skill. I don't. Trust is hard. It is hard to give. It is hard to earn. And it is hard to sustain.

EFFICIENT, EFFECTIVE, AND EMPOWERED

Humble self-confidence was key to President Bush's ability to build trust. He understood his strengths and his shortcomings. He sought out experts and listened to his team of advisors, without letting ego or fear (the greatest derailers of trust) get in his way.

As a result of the trust President Bush placed in his team, his administration ran with efficiency. Meetings started and ended on time, rather than droning on for hours. There was no need for workdays to extend late into the night. This efficiency was possible because the president empowered senior leadership to make decisions without micromanaging. Of course, there was a certain amount of deliberation and debate of issues, but the confidence President Bush placed in his advisors expedited progress.

Highly competent people make it easier for a leader to extend trust. President Bush surrounded himself with quality decision-makers, such as Karl Rove, Condoleezza Rice, Karen Hughes, and Colin Powell. There were also less-famous members of his staff. President Bush knew the name and valued the expertise of each person. His regard for and confidence in his staff increased their trust in him and led to extraordinary results.

The president's trust came with high expectations. He wanted his people to follow an orderly routine and be prepared with information and suggestions.

Punctuality was important. If you weren't early, you were late. If President Bush had a scheduled activity, like a bike ride, at 6:00 a.m., he'd be there by 5:50 a.m. Anyone showing up by 5:55 a.m. was late. I learned early on to arrive ready to go, fifteen minutes prior to scheduled meeting times. Punctuality was just one of the many areas in which President Bush had high expectations for those around him, but he led by example.

THE PRESIDENT'S MOST TRUSTED

Inarguably, President Bush trusted one person more than any other: the First Lady.

One day, I boarded Marine One with the president and Mrs. Bush for a quick ride to Camp David. Just prior to departing from the South Lawn of the White House, the president, wanting to ride his bike later, asked me what the weather was like there. From my personal experience, I recognized that Bush had four categories for rain. First, there was drizzle. Drizzle gave him no hesitation, as if it weren't raining at all. Next there was light rain. Light rain didn't require an umbrella, but covering the distance from the car to the front door might call for a quick jog. Then, there was plain ol' rain—an umbrella was needed. The last category was heavy rain, where it was flat out raining cats and dogs.

I asked for a SITREP from the Marine One controller on the ground at Camp David. He told me, "Light rain," and I relayed that to President Bush. The president looked skeptically out the window as we left Washington. The sun shone in a blue sky.

As we approached the landing zone at Camp David, the prop wash from the helicopter skewed our visibility.

"That's light rain?" the president teased.

"Yes, sir," I replied. Since I couldn't really tell, I had to go with what the controller had said.

He turned to Mrs. Bush. "Laura, is that light rain to you?"

She looked at him, then at me, and without glancing out of the window, she said, "Honey, that's light rain."

She flashed me a smile. It was just fun banter, but I appreciated her backup. One might argue the boss had spoken.

SAFETY TO DISAGREE

Most of the time, the president trusted us unquestioningly with day-to-day security measures. But he was human, as were we. Inevitably, he second-guessed some of our decisions.

President Bush was scheduled to take Marine One on another trip to Camp David for a day off and a much-anticipated bike ride, but the weather wasn't cooperating. The call was made to delay the flight.

"Let's go!" he said, expecting the helicopter to be waiting.

"Mr. President, look at the fog. You can't even see the Washington Monument. How do you expect a helicopter to get in here?" (I was comfortable giving such a candid and somewhat teasing remark because of the culture he'd created.)

Once the president took a moment to look outside, he immediately understood we'd have to wait. He gave me a sheepish grin.

Having the psychological safety to disagree with the president, regardless of his emotions, allowed me to serve him to the best of my abilities. If he had trusted my decisions less, my protection would have been worth less.

SAFETY TO LAUGH

One weekend, following another bike ride, I relaxed in my assigned cabin at Camp David. President Franklin D. Roosevelt and Prime Minister Winston Churchill were said to have planned the D-Day invasion from the porch of the same cabin. The history of foreign dignitaries that had stayed at Camp David and the negotiations accomplished there boggled my mind. I often thought of the magnitude of what had transpired in those hallowed spaces and marveled that my job afforded me the opportunity to be there and to watch current events unfold. On that particular day, I was having one of those "pinch me" moments.

The president's secretary interrupted my thoughts with a call to tell me that I needed to meet some officials at the front gate. *Playtime's over*, I thought.

I rode up on a golf cart and met a black, tinted SUV as it pulled into the highly secured compound. Two foreboding men in dark suits and opaque sunglasses stepped out of the car. I felt underdressed in my khakis and polo.

Representatives of the secretary of defense, the men confirmed my credentials and then made a big production of opening a briefcase, removing a soft case, opening the soft case to reveal a third case, and then unzipping the third case. From within the matryoshka-style set of cases, they finally revealed a manila envelope closed with a tamper-proof seal and stamped multiple times with red-lettered words: "FOR THE PRESIDENT'S EYES ONLY."

I immediately called the president's valet and headed over to President Bush's cabin, Aspen Lodge, to deliver the top-secret document as soon as the president was available.

Since we were at Camp David to celebrate President Bush's sixty-third birthday, I used the opportunity to deliver the gift the military aides had collectively purchased for him as well—a cigar lighter and some treats for the Bushes' pet Scottish terriers, Barney and Miss Beazley.

His eyes lit up as he opened the items, and he smiled as he passed them to the First Lady to see.

Next, I handed the president the manila envelope that had come that afternoon.

"It's from the secretary of defense," I said.

He looked confused. "Who?" he asked.

"Robert Gates," I answered.

"You don't think I know who my secretary of defense is?" the president said wryly.

I immediately realized my misstep.

The president had been unclear about receiving the package in such an unusual manner and at an unexpected time. I'd misunderstood his confusion.

My comment made the president sound dumb. And considering how the media was constantly trying to insult his intelligence, it could have been a sore topic for him. Though I knew firsthand that President Bush was anything but dumb (researchers estimated his IQ to be in the top 95th percentile of Americans),[22] he still could have punished my affront to his intellect with fire and brimstone (as MFB would have). Instead, he laughed and offered me the psychological safety to laugh too.

Government pomp could be intimidating, and procedures surrounding highly classified material could cause strain. It certainly wasn't a stress-free environment. At times—like when I showed up in khakis and a golf cart to meet a menacing SUV or when I insulted the president of the United States to his face—I questioned what I was doing there. But this small interaction, this shared moment of amusement and vulnerability, strengthened my feeling of belonging at work and deepened my level of fulfillment.

CREATIVE THINKING

The trust President Bush extended to his staff gave us the confidence and freedom to act in creative ways to achieve our missions. For instance, my good friend and fellow MILAIDE Mark Thompson was assigned the task of covertly moving the president from the White House to a combat zone in the Middle East for a visit at Christmastime. The ride to Andrews Air Force Base to board Air Force One took place in the middle of the night. They traveled in ordinary Suburbans through traffic—no flashing lights, no blocking of intersections. This meant that Mark, who was following in the SUV behind the president, and the others had to be on high alert and ready to improvise if needed.

At one stop light, a panhandler started to approach the president's window, though he had no idea who was in the vehicle. The Secret Service agent driving the car Mark rode in noticed the panhandler and quickly thought of a diversion, "Throw him some money."

Pockets were fished through, change discovered, and a hefty handful was passed Mark's way. Rolling down the window, Mark hucked the coins noisily behind the panhandler and away from the president's car. The man quickly turned to collect the money, never realizing who was in the vehicle he'd approached. The light turned green, and the SUVs safely continued toward Andrews.

The danger of that moment didn't come from the panhandler himself but from the possibility of word getting out that the president was on the move. Such intel would have jeopardized President Bush's security as he traveled to a war zone.

When a culture doesn't offer its people psychological safety, they stick to rule books and avoid creative decision-making for fear of retribution. Luckily, the culture in Bush's administration encouraged initiative. There was no official protocol for the situation Mark and the others encountered, but knowing that they had the president's trust gave them the confidence to think creatively and follow through on a plan to create a distraction.

Nothing in Mark's MILAIDE job description said he needed to be on top of the micro-level threats. However, the Bush administration's culture fostered love and a desire to go beyond the job description without a second thought. We helped each other, and we helped the boss—no questions asked.

AN UNNERVING MISSION

In 2008, I was tasked with escorting the First Lady on a clandestine trip to Afghanistan—an active war zone. Knowing the president was depending on me, in coordination with the Secret Service, to keep his wife safe was validating and beyond anything I'd ever been entrusted with.

I couldn't have felt more honored. I hoped to prove the president's belief in me was well placed. More importantly, I cared deeply about the First Lady and wanted to keep her safe. Mrs. Bush's kindness and knack for making everyone around her feel valued endeared her to all of us and made us fiercely protective of her.

The trip was logistically difficult. As the on-scene operational commander, I was responsible for planning and coordinating with Combined Joint Task Force 101, the Secret Service, and the embassy. Some of the upper brass at Bagram Air Base wanted to transport the First Lady and her support staff in H-60 helicopters. We'd need ten to twelve of the smaller helicopters to get the job done. I suspected that a four-star general was thinking more about sitting next to Mrs. Bush in a helicopter than he was the overall security of the mission.

The attention so many helicopters would draw worried me. The pilots on the ground at Bagram had voiced their concerns and said the larger H-53s should be used instead. Fewer birds in the air would garner less suspicion. I conferred with multiple experts, including Assistant Special Agent in Charge Dan Donahue. Our concerns were brought to the top brass, and our arguments were convincing. We went with the H-53s.

The visit was a success, and I returned the First Lady back to the White House unscathed. I'd be lying if I said I wasn't relieved at the end of the mission. I'd stood in the Oval Office with the president and foreign heads of state, and I'd been an executive officer of a nuclear submarine during tense missions—but riding a helicopter into the hills of Afghanistan with the wife of the president was the most unnerving experience I'd ever had.

I was thrilled to have carried out the mission to the best of my abilities. I also realized that the psychological safety the Bushes had created extended beyond their direct influence. That safety had given me the confidence to disagree with a top leader and speak up for what I felt was right based on the expert feedback I had received. Who knows what would have happened if we'd gone with the smaller helicopters? Maybe nothing. Or maybe something really bad.

I wholeheartedly believe that the Bushes' habits of empowering people led directly to good decision-making and positive outcomes in that moment and many others.

From left to right: Murphy's parents, Daniel and Maureen Murphy, President George W. Bush, and Cmdr. Robert Roncska

EXTREME LEADERSHIP

There are times in your life when things come full circle. Two years earlier, I'd been on the *La Jolla* with members of SEAL Delivery Vehicle Team One when they'd received news of their fallen brothers. Now, I was given the somber but unforgettable privilege of participating in a ceremony to honor one of those very men.

When twenty-nine-year-old Lieutenant Michael Murphy and his team found themselves in Afghanistan surrounded by enemy forces, Murphy, already wounded, left his covered position to gain a better satellite phone signal to call in rescue support for his comrades. Murphy acted "unhesitatingly and with complete disregard for his own life."[23] His fight for a better position despite the blanket of gunfire meant his certain death. At one point, Murphy dropped the phone after being shot in the back, but he picked it back up to complete the call. He even said "thank you" when signing off. Murphy returned to his covered position and continued to fight, but ultimately succumbed to his injuries.[24]

Danny Dietz and Matt Axelson, who'd also lost their lives in the battle, had been posthumously honored the year before with the Navy Cross. On this day, we were gathered to award Murphy for his bravery and sacrifice with our nation's highest military decoration, the Medal of Honor.

I held the wooden box containing the hallowed gold star as President Bush presented it to the parents of Lieutenant Michael Murphy. The mission's lone survivor, Marcus Luttrell, was there too. There wasn't a dry eye in the crowd.

I was reminded of the strong bonds I'd witnessed while interacting with the SEALs on the *La Jolla*. From their brotherhood—formed during the atrocities of war—grew deep, self-sacrificing loyalty.

Though I never met Murphy personally, his actions during his final battle spoke volumes: He was a man willing to give his life for those serving under him. He was a next-level leader who demonstrated why the SEALs are so successful: they lead and love to the extreme.

BACK TO SEA

As my time at the White House wound down, it became time to submit my preferences for command. My current detailer, Jeff Trussler, reached out to tell me about upcoming options. Given my experience, Jeff wanted to put my name in the running to become the commander of a Virginia-class nuclear submarine. It gave me a lot to think about.

The thought of commanding my own ship got me excited. Make no mistake, whatever assignments a naval officer has had up to that point, commanding one's own submarine is the pinnacle of one's career.

However, I had mixed feelings. I was currently serving the president of the United States. Each day I walked stately halls filled with our nation's history. I was surrounded by a fantastic team of individuals who demonstrated an ideal mix of camaraderie and professionalism. Though I had an exceedingly demanding schedule and regular travel requirements, I was not away from my family for months at a time, as I would be on a sub. I got to be home with my kids most nights. I got to watch movies, read books, and tuck them in. My daughter didn't cling to me each time she heard my keys jingle. Life was really good.

Stephanie and I talked about where we would like to be stationed and what a sea tour would mean to the family. We weighed the pros and cons of each duty station as we contemplated the task of building a new home for our kids. Military service can take a toll on the entire family. My wife and kids needed to be all in. In this case, they were. We pushed forward to face the reality of life at sea once again.

ASPIRATIONS

Soon, I found myself named the commanding officer of the USS *Texas* (SSN-775). It could not have been more apropos: Laura Bush was its sponsor and had christened the submarine. It was as though I wasn't leaving the Bushes' service after all. Navy tradition says that a sponsor is the heart of a ship, and there was no one with more heart than the First Lady.

Before officially taking command of the *Texas*, I spent a lot of time thinking about my experience as a submariner. *What were the high and low points? What could I learn from my past? Who did I want to emulate? What legacy did I want to leave?*

As I thought about how I wished to lead, I made some conscious decisions:

I wanted to be like my dad, sacrificing for the good of others and working hard to give generously of my time and talents.

I wanted to create a culture like Grooms had. Those who served under my command should feel a sense of belonging and purpose, know that they were highly valued, and believe themselves capable of great things. They ought to be extended second chances and the support and tools they needed to succeed. My ship had to be a safe haven for sailors to speak up and think creatively. My team should be able to learn and grow while ensuring the safety of the ship and those we were there to protect.

I wanted to be like Howes, listening deeply to the concerns of my sailors and soliciting their ideas. By recognizing my strengths and weaknesses and inviting others to fill in the gaps, I hoped to create a dynamic team with a culture of openness—a team with the tenacity to confront my authority when necessary. I wanted us to be authentic, vulnerable, and transparent.

Like President and Mrs. Bush, I hoped to foster a sense of belonging. I wanted my sailors to feel like they were part of our ship's family and, more importantly, my family.

I wanted to be compassionate and charismatic, to be an advocate for my crew, to extend and receive trust, to create a culture of psychological safety, and to strive for and demand excellence.

I wanted a lot!

I'd been privileged to serve under some great leaders. I intended to follow in their footsteps to the best of my ability. With this time of reflection, my vision for my role as commanding officer crystallized. I felt eager to begin my duty on the *Texas*, and hopeful that I'd be able to re-create the magic of the best cultures I'd experienced. I knew if I did it right, incredible results would follow.

PART FOUR:
APPLYING LEADERSHIP LESSONS

― CHAPTER 13 ―

THE EFFECTS OF APATHY

"I have a very strong feeling that the opposite of love is not hate—it's apathy. It's not giving a damn."

—LEO BUSCAGLIA

Before I assumed command on the *Texas*, I was required to complete another year of intense, specialized schooling. My excitement built during this period of study as I imagined my command. I also felt uncertainty and even fear at the magnitude of what I was about to undertake. My worries related to me and my abilities, not the boat. So when I became aware that the *Texas* didn't have the greatest performance reputation, I didn't think much about it. I failed to grasp the difficulty of the situation or the work that would be necessary to pull the *Texas* back from the brink.

As I mentioned earlier, the navy has never had any accidents related to the use of nuclear power because of the high-reliability standards and protocols Admiral Rickover established. It was these safety standards, or lack of them, that fueled talk about the *Texas*—chatter I conveniently overlooked.

My reality check would come as soon as I stepped on board.

Protocol required me to spend my first thirty days on the *Texas* with the outgoing commander. The overlap would allow me the time to acclimate and to observe and interact with the team without the responsibility of decision-making.

The thirty days of observation were a gift. They allowed me to reflect further on the leadership lessons I had learned and to get to know the crew. The many conversations I had with the sailors during that time were my favorite part.

However, my eyes were also opened to numerous concerns. I was astonished by the lax attitude and general chaos on board. It became apparent how much hard work it would take to get this submarine turned around.

CAUSE FOR CONCERN

One example of this alarming laxity occurred during an engine room flooding drill I observed. In a submarine, an intake of water can be a death sentence. The water pressure at great depths magnifies the speed of flooding. It is crucial that the water is contained and the submarine has the propulsion necessary to bring the ship to the surface.

For a flooding drill, automatic closure of the oversized intake valves is initiated. This isolates the ship from all significant hull openings, allowing a team to find the leak as soon as possible and stop the inrush of water. Once the leak is found, specific portals need to be reopened quickly to provide enough water flow to cool the system. Then a feed pump needs to be started to replenish the generators and propel the ship to the surface.

The informality and lack of urgency exhibited by the crew during the drill was shocking.

Because of the casual pace during the exercise, both steam generators had been allowed to boil down, inching closer to disastrously low levels that would make it impossible to maintain propulsion. The time for correction was running out.

An order was given by the engineering officer of the watch, "Electrical Operator, start number two main feed pump."

Without confirming the order with the required repeat-back, the sailor gave a wrong command over the communication circuit to the engineering watch supervisor, "Start number *one* main feed pump."

This erroneous order was repeated back on a microphone in the maneuvering space, "Start number one main feed pump, aye."

The team in the maneuvering began to shout, "No, no, no! Number two, number two!"

The confusion in maneuvering escalated. The rest of the engine room watch standers joined the chorus, "Not pump one, pump two!"

It was too late. The distraction from the incorrect order kept the throttle man from watching the steam generator's water levels. The electrical operator started pump number one, and the entire system tripped offline. It was not designed to support the load from the starboard side of the electrical distribution system. Fortunately, the drill monitor directed the throttles to be shut immediately, preventing further water loss and damage to the steam generator and stopping the drill. Had he not done so, the boat would have lost propulsion and been unable to surface. In a real flood, this would have had catastrophic consequences, similar to those of the USS *Thresher* in 1963, when all hands were lost during dive trials after the failure of joint seals along a saltwater piping system.

The strict formality of the military system exists to save lives. The repeating of orders is both a confirmation and an opportunity to course correct, if necessary. Neglecting this basic yet vital practice puts a ship and crew in danger.

On a nuclear submarine, simulations are a regular part of life. It is vital that everyone on board knows how to respond to a host of emergency situations. Running drills creates muscle memory and improves reactions in such adverse circumstances. Drills are also a good measure of competency. The lack of standards and communication I observed during the flooding simulation was a clear indication the *Texas* was unsafe and not ready for a real emergency.

And this was just the tip of the iceberg.

After my thirty days of observation, my role as CO began in earnest with a series of several short underways. I would sleep on the ship the night before an underway and rise around 6:00 a.m. when the crew was required to be back on board. I would awaken to find them in total disarray. They'd be scrambling to check items off their pre-underway list that could easily have been attended to the night before or rummaging around looking for equipment that had not been properly stowed.

I would hear "Where are the harnesses?" or "Where is my relief?" echoing throughout the sub.

It was total confusion.

I quickly learned that the level of disorganization during underway mornings correlated directly with the level of dysfunction within a particular department. The worse the chaos, the worse the dysfunction.

Stepping in to fix the situation in real-time was like putting out fires and felt virtually impossible. Later, when I tried to uncover the root cause of the pandemonium with division leaders and department heads, I'd be met with statements like "Yeah, it's messed up" but no real answers or solutions. It was another indicator of the magnitude of our broken culture on board the *Texas*.

A LIST OF DEFICIENCIES

The time came to prepare for a home-port shift from New London to Pearl Harbor. During our transit, we would be going under the North Pole, so we also needed to get the ship certified for Arctic operations. In preparation for both the home-port shift and the certification to conduct the transit, we had to run an endless string of drills. We also needed to ensure that required maintenance, supplies, and certifications were up to date. Squadron command would be looking at everything. All boxes needed to be checked and rechecked for us to receive the green light for the upcoming mission.

While I was in my stateroom attending to some paperwork, a knock sounded on my door. The weapons officer of the squadron was on board to complete his inspection for one of our certifications. He was kind enough to give me a heads-up before going to the commodore, my direct boss, with his findings. The officer explained that six months earlier—prior to my time on the *Texas*—he had given the ship a list of deficiencies to correct. He'd just found that no action had been taken in the interim.

I asked for the officer's report and identified several issues that could be readily fixed. The first involved expiring weapons qualifications for a number of sailors. Though the crew of nuclear submarines don't typically experience hand-to-hand combat, they must be ready to do so if a threat arises. When in port—especially a foreign port—sailors take turns standing watch. Proper certification is required for those guarding the sub, and several of them had certifications set to expire during our underway period. This was an easy fix.

The second low-hanging fruit I identified was an inadequate inventory of protective equipment. We were missing some of the basics, such as helmets. A quick call to the supply officer could take care of this.

A broken temperature gauge in our storage room was one of several simple maintenance items on the officer's list. The climate below the sea can change drastically, depending on the surrounding waters. Munitions are not as forgiving as the human body, so climate control in a storage room is vital. Our temperature gauge was out of calibration, and there was no excuse.

The list of items needing corrective action or preventative maintenance was long and unnerving. The worst part was knowing that no one in the entire chain of command had taken steps to address even the most basic of these deficiencies. It was yet another indicator of our greatest underlying problem: apathy.

What made matters worse was the finger-pointing that transpired as I attempted to uncover the root cause of our issues. Instead of an open dialogue, I found defensiveness and a lack of accountability, with no effort to identify missing protocols or offer solutions. The crew lacked respect for one another, undervalued nuclear navy standards, and demonstrated a generalized apathy toward excellence. It was the trifecta of a dangerous culture.

Unsurprisingly, we also had low retention. The high level of transfer requests was a clear indicator of the dissatisfaction felt by the sailors on the *Texas*. We were ranked at the bottom of the entire squadron, and it wasn't a fun place to be.

RISING PRESSURE

I was understandably nervous as we prepared to take this new two-billion-dollar class of submarine into frigid Arctic waters underneath the polar ice cap. What I had observed up to this point had not instilled any confidence in our ability to succeed. Rather, I felt worried about the safety of my crew.

The *Texas* would navigate to the North Pole via the formidable waters of the Bering Strait, the gateway between the Arctic and Pacific Oceans. The Bering Strait separates the United States and Russia by just over fifty miles. The seabed lies only one hundred feet below the surface at the strait's shallowest point. We knew our adversaries played in the region, and we had reports that they were eager to hunt down a new Virginia-class submarine.

Political pressure on our ship continued to escalate. The navy was eager to test the capabilities of the Virginia-class submarine and certify it for Arctic operations. If we were successful, then any other submarine of the same class could travel these waters without restrictions. It's not an overstatement to say that national security depended on the outcome of our mission.

In a meeting with squadron command, the commodore poked me in the chest and said, "The entire submarine community is counting on you. Get this ship Arctic-certified."

"Yes, sir!" I replied—as if there were any other response.

I anxiously moved forward with preparations for our departure. The daily arctic imagery reports showed that the growth rate of ice was faster than normal that year. We would be navigating under a growing barrier that could decrease our ability to break through to the surface. I had no choice but to expedite our already-aggressive departure date.

I was confident in the nuclear power of the submarine that would allow us to operate under the ice for an extended period of time without surfacing. However, the mission brought with it three major concerns. First, the low temperatures of the Arctic water could cause condensation and turn our high-tech engine room into a rainforest. Water might seep into microprocessors and circuitry, shorting out the power and leaving us to run on battery backup. Battery power, however, lasts for only a few hours. If we got caught in an area with thick ice and no way to surface before our battery ran out or reactor was restored, it would mean certain death.

Next, we would be traveling through an area called "the iceberg factory"—the same waters where the Titanic met its fate. The only way to navigate the area safely would be with active sonar. Unfortunately, our adversaries would be listening for our sonar.

The last and, for me, biggest issue was our apathetic culture. With our problem of indifference and failure to consistently follow Rickover's long-established safety standards, we would never be able to accomplish our mission unscathed.

Our culture cried out for an immediate overhaul. I needed to figure out how to fix the root cause of this apathy.

CHAPTER 14

TIME FOR AN INTERVENTION

"A team fused by trust and purpose is much more potent. They can improvise a coordinated response to dynamic, real-time developments."

—GENERAL STANLEY MCCHRYSTAL

To prepare for the monumental task we were facing, I began to dig deeper to find the cause of our dysfunction. From what I'd gathered, the crew received frequent verbal lashings and landed in captain's mast for even minor transgressions. The CO doled out punishments, which might range from extra duty to reduced pay or rations. The result of a captain's mast could be placed on sailors' permanent records, negatively impacting their career opportunities down the road.

I was surprised to learn that the previous command used captain's mast as a primary tool for discipline. Sometimes it is warranted, but excessive punishment can be devastating to morale, improvement, and culture. It certainly doesn't get to the root cause of the problem.

In order to address incidents and safety concerns effectively, I went hunting for documents that could help me better understand the processes and procedures on board. I found that major occurrences, like a reactor safety issue, only had typical root-cause identification and corrective action. In the past, command had addressed lack of knowledge and failed procedural compliance with more training but had not reported further follow-through. As a result, small but overlooked inefficiencies compounded.

We were in dire need of process improvement and transparency. The team needed a win, and I wanted to give them a reason to celebrate. Unfortunately, in order to demonstrate the type of positive and productive response I wanted the crew to get used to, I first needed something to go wrong. I didn't have long to wait.

AN INCIDENT TO REPORT

Aware of our deficiencies and all that was at stake, I slept on board the nights we had a reactor startup. One night, the inevitable happened. A knock on my stateroom door at 2:00 a.m. woke me.

"Captain! We had an instrument malfunction during the reactor startup while latching control rods, and we had to SCRAM the reactor."

Essentially, a SCRAM terminates the fission reaction by use of a kill switch, causing an immediate shutdown. In the early days of nuclear reactors, the "kill switch" was a man who used an axe to cut a rope and initiate this process. This axe-wielding professional was called the safety control rod axe man (SCRAM for short).

The good news was that the crew had followed procedure properly for a reactor equipment malfunction.

Unfortunately, during corrective action to replace the malfunctioning reactor plant drawer, the frontline sailors failed to set the proper drawer settings and conduct the appropriate retests. No one in the chain of command, including me, backed up the sailors' corrective action.

The engineering department completed all the required paperwork but missed the drawer-setting error. The engineering officer requested permission to conduct a valve lineup and reactor pre-startup in preparation for the reactor startup, and I granted it. Each of us missed the mistake, but as the highest-ranking officer, I held the ultimate responsibility.

By chance, during the pre-startup procedure, the squadron chief reactor control assistant started reviewing the retest paperwork for the failed reactor drawer and found the error. He immediately left the ship to report his findings.

In the nuclear world, this oversight was a big deal. Though the chance of a reactor accident was small because of redundancies and many other control rods, even a slight chance of an accident was unacceptable. Every redundancy needed to be in place and functioning. We had failed in supervision and backup.

Soon, a yeoman approached me and said, "The commodore is on the line for you, sir."

A sinking feeling came over me. Already facing political and time pressures, I steeled myself for a well-deserved rebuke about our performance.

"I want to review everything," the commodore said. His concern was understandable.

The entire squadron staff descended on the ship like FBI agents conducting a raid. Nothing was off-limits. But after three days of intense investigation, the commodore decided the event was merely a consequence of a bad day. He even asked me whether or not I cared to write an incident report.

A report would take considerable time to write and would have to be submitted directly to Naval Reactors (the four-star admiral who headed the office of the same name and led the entire nuclear navy). It would draw the attention of many critical eyes and leave naval leadership wondering whether Roncska could deliver. It might even damage my career or the careers of the officers I worked with.

Nevertheless, I knew in my heart we had a problem. The mistake stemmed from a poor culture, though I didn't know how to prove it and wasn't sure how to change it. I'd only been in command of the *Texas* for three months, but I couldn't continue to blame the past administration for current problems.

I needed to set an example of transparency. I needed to put pride aside and ask for help from the squadron. The ultimate safety of my crew was at stake.

I took a deep breath and said, "Commodore, I'm writing an incident report."

This ship had a pattern that we desperately needed to break. Six months prior, under the previous command, the crew had experienced a similar near-miss event. Leadership at the time had responded with more training and monitoring, without ever addressing the culture of the crew. After reading and reflecting on many reports, I concluded that these accidents grew from indifference, not a lack of practice. The crew didn't care about the ship because the ship didn't care about them. Sailors didn't feel valued or like part of a family. There was no trust, and there certainly was no magic.

The summary of my incident report began writing itself:

> *After a rigorous review of this mishap and a near-exact same incident six months prior, the corrective actions then were ineffective and not warranted for this most recent event. The root cause is the culture of this crew. This ship does not take care of these sailors, and these sailors are not taking care of this ship.*

Despite my fears about reporting the event, I later heard from someone on staff at Naval Reactors that one of the top brass had remarked after reading the report, "Roncska gets it."

That feedback gave me hope and confidence. I wasn't alone. Others in the fleet recognized that culture could be a significant problem.

WORK TO DO

I wanted my crew to feel safe to demonstrate the questioning attitude critical to a nuclear submarine. Unfortunately, what transpired during the squadron's review of our reactor control equipment proved my leaders were mired in apathy. When an investigator couldn't locate the retesting documentation for several pieces of equipment, he assumed the required checks hadn't occurred.

Missing the retest of one drawer was bad enough; failing to retest multiple pieces of equipment would have evinced incredible recklessness and incompetence. I found it difficult to believe that the crew had skipped all of those mandatory procedures. However, my officers were so accustomed to getting beaten down by the previous command that they didn't bother to voice their objections. They just prepared to shoulder more blame. The engineer, the reactor controls assistant officer, and the reactor controls leading chief petty officer all told me it was possible that they had missed the needed retests. Thankfully, a first-class petty officer objected and came through with the truth.

"I think I know what happened," the petty officer said. "The documentation that referenced other paperwork was missed."

I was thrilled the sailor had spoken up, and I praised him for his gumption. His input led us to documentation showing we *had* properly tested all reactor control equipment. It felt like a big win.

Building on the momentum, we began investigating past issues. I wanted to rid my team of apathy and work together to increase overall safety. It was time to focus on standards.

My crew deserved a clear understanding of my expectations, so I went to my stateroom one evening and drafted my command philosophy (see appendix). Upon completing the document, I had personal conversations with each individual on board. I clarified my thinking on subjects such as pride, competence, and respect to every sailor and officer. I required each shipmate to read the philosophy, acknowledge the expectations of compliance, and sign a commitment to behave in accordance with expectations. Making this commitment became a part of our onboarding process as well.

It ensured that everyone was working from the same level of understanding. It also established clear standards of accountability, which gave me a foundation for developmental conversations. There was little excuse for violating principles that everyone had discussed and committed to in such a way. Once I'd established expectations, I looked for ways to elevate standards. I wanted opportunities to show corrective action could be positive and free of punishment.

CREW TOP THREE

My takeaway from my root cause analysis of our incident was twofold: the crew didn't follow the proper procedure during maintenance due to apathy, and the primary cause of the apathy was a lack of love. I resolved to build trust and purpose with love. I wanted each member of the crew to feel that I valued and cared for them, even at a personal cost to me. I would make sure they all knew I loved them as if they were my family.

It was time to put my ideals into action. It was time for our first Crew Top Three. Following in the footsteps of Captain Howes, I directed the chief of the boat to muster the team topside.

Skeptical faces stared back, but I could see a glimmer of interest as I thanked them for joining me. There was a cautious receptiveness as I explained the Crew Top Three process.

"Tell me, what are your top three concerns? They could be anything from parking to working conditions to the softness of the toilet paper . . . I care about you and the pebbles in your shoes."

Silence.

I didn't know what to expect after I dismissed the sailors. Likely, they didn't either.

Later that day, I sat at my desk tackling the pile of Crew Top Three responses that had come in. The theme that quickly emerged astonished me. Many of the sailors said they'd made requests before but had received no response or corrective action. One sailor discussed a travel expense that had not been reimbursed for over nine months. That sailor's government credit card now had delinquent payments, which negatively affected his credit score.

Several men expressed frustration over the lack of computers on our brand-new submarine—computers that were essential for work processes and studying for qualification exams. Sailors were required to continue their professional education. Not only did they have to study in their off-duty time, but they also had to do so on the ship since the majority of the subject matter was sensitive or classified and could not be viewed at home. That made it necessary for sailors to spend two or more hours studying on board after their shift. With our inadequate number of computers, men found themselves wasting their off-duty time on the ship, hanging around, waiting for a computer. It was horrible for morale and a clear indication to the sailors that command didn't value their time.

The lack of computers was not the fault of the IT chief. He was one of the best in the fleet. Unfortunately, he was missing the support he needed to get through the supply procurement process. I was determined to help him break through the barriers he had encountered.

LOVE AND ACTION

I had mixed emotions as I read through the Crew Top Three responses. I was elated to be taking first steps toward fixing our problems. However, I was beyond upset that we'd treated the crew in this way.

I called the COB, Rory Wohlgemuth, who led our enlisted crew—truly the center of our ship. The COB had pure intentions and did what he could for morale, trying to maintain order and serve as the crew's big brother. I knew how important his influence would be in helping us turn our culture around. I didn't blame the COB, but we had to be vulnerable and admit we'd failed to fully grasp the impact these neglected items had on crew morale and safety.

"COB, I'm disappointed that we didn't know about these issues sooner. This can't happen again. Muster the entire crew topside."

Rory grabbed the ship-wide announcing system, "*Texas*, report topside."

As I stood before them that same afternoon, the crew faced me with slumped shoulders and bowed heads. They appeared to be waiting for a beating. It was clear I hadn't won their trust yet.

I stared at them and after a long pause said, "I just reviewed your Crew Top Three responses and realize now that I have let you down. I am deeply sorry about this. I failed you by not asking sooner. I will do my best not to let it happen again! You are family, and I love you."

Not many military leaders say "I love you" to those under their command. However, I wanted my shipmates to know how I truly felt. I could think of no stronger word than "love."

"I called the commodore, and we're getting thirty new computers today," I said.

The crew looked totally confused. It was clear many were still expecting to get yelled at. Some looked up when I mentioned the computers—a couple even smiled—but everyone remained quiet. I knew trust would take time; still, this was a beginning.

FIXING ISSUES

By the end of the week, we managed to rectify several more issues. In the following months, we uncovered many major and minor problems through the Crew Top Three process. I was able to fix housing and pay matters, certification awards, scheduling discrepancies, and work-life balance issues that kept the crew from important time with their families. Backing my words with action was the first step in building trust and cultivating a family-work culture of love.

Once sailors began to notice problems were being addressed, more of them felt comfortable and emboldened to bring additional concerns to light. Petty Officer John Deming held a special place in my heart because of his willingness to speak up. He often uncovered critical issues, such as lax certification standards that left gaps in the care of the ship. One of Deming's duties was to line up the system for weekly battery charges. He pointed out that he was the only one on board qualified to do this, which meant the ship was vulnerable when he was away. We quickly rectified this by raising the number of sailors required to be certified in this area and by creating a system of accountability to maintain those certifications. This discovery led us to identify more areas in which qualifications were lagging. Upping our level of various certifications not only raised standards in many areas and increased the safety of the ship, but it also enhanced the service records of the sailors.

A PROTECTIVE SEA DOG

We communicated our successful solutions and shared our failures during our monthly Crew Top Three. Whenever I could, I layered in the purpose of our work, the value of what had been accomplished, or the contribution of an individual. I felt protective of my crew and would advocate on their behalf. As a veteran "sea dog," I wanted my actions to show that no one messes with my "pups."

During our preparation period, we had squadron personnel on board conducting inspections as well as maintenance. The squadron IT technician wanted to do a software upgrade, but the ship's engineer didn't want to risk any software issues until the reactor had shut down. The IT person didn't wish to wait and decided to go over the engineer's head. I was incensed. I immediately kicked the IT technician off the ship, much to the dismay of my boss when word reached him. The story quickly spread throughout the *Texas*, and the level of trust rose as a consequence. "Don't mess with the pups" became a favorite mantra.

AS SIMPLE AS SHUFFLEBOARD

My attempts to improve culture in those early days included encouragement of off-duty fun. Facing intense pressure to begin our big transit, we worked long hours to complete our preparations. Most of our families were gone, having already made the move to our new home port of Hawaii. During the little time we had off, many crew members visited a local establishment to play shuffleboard and throw back a few beers.

A rumor surfaced that I claimed to be a world-class shuffleboard player whom no one could beat. In reality, I was average at best, but I could be a bit competitive even on something like rock, paper, scissors. If I beat someone in a game, I'd announce it to the whole ship. It was all in good fun, though.

Andrew Shelly, one of our enlisted electrician mates, could not let the outrageous shuffleboard rumor go unanswered. He organized a ship-wide tournament and advertised the event like a politician stumping for votes. The smack talk reached epic heights as teams quickly signed up for the bracket. A spark of camaraderie began to ignite.

On the evening of the tournament, a capacity crowd watched the *Texas* crew battle it out in a smoke-filled room, with flowing beer and a ruckus of hoots and hollers. After some extremely close matches, the championship game came down to two teams: an electrician mate and a chief versus a lieutenant and me.

As the game began, my adrenalin pumped. I yelled every time my partner or I had a good shot. I'd try to distract our opponents on their turn by getting close to their throwing hand or in their ear. They didn't respond with the boisterous sparring we expected. Instead, they remained calm and collected, showering us with compliments.

"Hey, that was a great shot!"

"Nice one!"

"Wow, that was awesome!"

Their excessive congratulations were a sneaky way to throw me off my game, and it worked. I started missing easy shots. My opponents were absolutely living rent-free in my head. They won, no doubt because of their brilliant strategy, and deservedly so.

On that night, the *Texas* family was born. Andrew's organization of the casual tournament sparked some things we had been missing: fun, a sense of accomplishment, and fellowship.

Playing together was a bonding experience—even Douglas MacArthur would agree. When the general served as superintendent of West Point, he said about cadet athletics, "Upon the fields of friendly strife are sown the seeds that on other days, on other fields, will bear the fruits of victory."[25]

Andrew's effort was one of the catalysts for our success. Something as simple as shuffleboard helped to unify us.

A TROUBLING TREND

I still highly encourage casual bonding over a friendly game of shuffleboard, cribbage, or any other competitive endeavor. However, my love of a party-like atmosphere may not have always set the best example.

One night, a small group of officers and I were headed to the movies, planning to call it an early night afterwards. We drove down the street, joking, laughing, and enjoying one of the last nights ashore before our long underway would confine us to the *Texas*. Off to my left, I caught sight of flashing blue lights in my peripheral vision. I didn't think much of it, especially considering we were passing a bar. But when I looked closer, I saw some familiar faces. My laughter abruptly stopped.

We turned around and pulled up behind the police vehicle. As I approached the scene, I could see two of my men with a pair of policemen. One of the sailors was taking a sobriety test by "walking the line." My heart sank.

I identified myself and asked the officer conducting the test how I could offer support. At first, he wasn't interested in what I had to say. But the other policeman pulled me aside and spoke with me. I explained to him that I was the sailors' commanding officer and wanted to help. Once the test finished, and the tipsy sailor had clearly failed, the two officers conferred and returned to me.

"Will you take care of this?" they asked. "Make sure he gets home and take appropriate action?" I assured them that I would hold my men accountable. The officers released them both into my custody.

I interrogated the men further. I was disappointed to find that not only was the inebriated sailor well above the legal limit, but he had convinced the other, sober sailor to allow him to test drive his new large truck. The sober sailor showed poor judgment and permitted the drunk one to take the wheel.

I was angry, disgusted, and relieved all at once.

With the police officers gone, I was responsible for the sailors' discipline. I made it clear to the sober sailor that his actions were unacceptable.

I expected my team to speak up and protect one another. His complicity could have cost lives that night. The other sailor's punishment would be meted out after he sobered up. In the meantime, both were escorted to the ship and returned safely to their bunks.

I took time that night to reflect and consider my next steps. But first, I had to look in the mirror and consider my part in this. I'd encouraged the crew in off-duty fun at a drinking establishment while many of us were geographical bachelors. In most cases, people behaved appropriately, but not that night.

I realized I had failed to speak up when I'd noticed a troubling trend earlier. The blood alcohol limit for a DUI on base was lower than the one in town. Several senior enlisted made a practice of parking off base, drinking at the chief's club, and having a duty driver take them to their cars. They made no secret of this, and although it wasn't breaking any law, I didn't think it set a good example. Yet, I failed to say anything.

I had the fate of the inebriated sailor in my hands. I could take him to captain's mast and possibly end his career. It might hurt his marriage too, as I knew his wife had a hard-and-fast rule against drunk driving. Since there was no arrest, I had no obligation to report the incident to squadron. Therefore, I could handle this internally, show him grace, and risk that my actions would fail to prevent another incident.

Out of love and concern for his future, I did the latter. The next morning, I gathered the entire crew topside again. I was completely open about what had happened, though it was uncomfortable for the individuals involved. I had decided that the entire crew must sign an agreement not to drive if they'd had anything at all to drink. They hated that, of course.

Then, I admitted to the crew that I had contributed to the problem by encouraging social time centered around drinking. I promised to do better, and I asked them to do the same. For the two offending sailors, I assigned extra work as further punishment.

My gamble paid off. When the crew saw that I took ownership of the situation, it helped me gain their trust. The sailor who had failed the sobriety test never had another incident. He served his country honorably and went on to have an amazing career. His wife—who was also the *Texas*'s ombudsman, helping families navigate the ups and downs of submarine life—was so appreciative of the second chance her husband had received.

RAISING STANDARDS

The navy standard at the time called for random drug testing of 5 percent of the crew. I thought that, with such a low chance of getting tested, many sailors might roll the dice. I told the squadron we planned to test 20 percent. It was my hope that increasing the probability their name would be called would prevent sailors from gambling with drug use. I loved them too much to see that happen.

Unfortunately, my attempts to deter drug use through high standards didn't work 100 percent of the time. In the navy, drug use is punished by separation from the service. I believed in this philosophy and upheld the standard. Though I had other ways to address my team's minor infractions, I also had to make them accountable for seriously bad choices. The few times I had to hold a captain's mast for drug use resulted in the sailors' separation. Luckily, I was able to stay well below the average of ten captain's masts per year by staying involved and confronting concerns with early intervention.

I hoped to inspire the crew with the same vision I had. I'd often say something like, "We can never lose sight of the fact that we serve on the most complex warship in the world, which spends most of its time operating hundreds of feet beneath the sea. We are highly trained, but we must always strive for improvement. We either get better or worse; we don't stay the same. I do not ask for perfection. However, I do demand that you give me your best effort, and I will do the same. Together we can make *Texas* the best submarine in the fleet."

Part of my weekly routine included announcements over the intercom for the entire crew. I used this scheduled time to highlight the good work taking place throughout the ship. To fuel my announcements, I required each leader to give me a daily note card with celebratory moments to recognize. It was fun to be able to say things like: "Thank you Petty Officer Smith for fixing the diesel generator and helping us get underway on time," or "Congratulations to Petty Officer Jones for completing his quartermaster of the watch certification." It was even better when I saw that sailor later in the day and could look him in the eyes and shake his hand.

AN INTEGRAL PART

I continued my mission to show appreciation to my sailors throughout my tour. Once, while on deployment, I was walking through the wardroom and passed the mess specialist, Jeremy Fitch, on his hands and knees, cleaning the floor. I thought of the hardworking cook on the *Asheville* and the way Grooms had praised him. I knew what I needed to do.

"What are you doing?" I asked.

Jeremy stopped and looked around at his work. "You know, Captain, just cleaning."

"Come with me," I said, motioning with my finger.

I took him to the control room and pointed to the screen. "You see that? Do you know what that is?"

Jeremy looked and thought. "No, sir," he finally said, "I have no idea."

I explained to him the type of foreign submarine we were tracking and walked him through the delicate nature of our business. I then said, "You're an integral part of our success. You know why?"

Jeremy shrugged, unsure of where the conversation was headed.

"All those meals you make," I told Jeremy. "Number one, the crew knows they're safe because you're careful about sanitation. The food is also healthy and tasty. You keep morale high. We found that sub because the crew is engaged, and they're engaged because you take care of them. We can't do this without you."

I knew my message hit home when I later observed the interaction between Fitch and a visiting admiral at lunch during a brief stop in Yokosuka, Japan. When the admiral asked, "Do you find your role important to the mission?"

Jeremy answered with confidence, "Yes, sir! I know my cooking and cleaning directly impact the morale of the crew, which contributes to our mission. And sanitation affects safety—which is also part of mission success."

NON-NEGOTIABLES

The navy has many traditions and rites of passage, even some barbaric ones that should not take place under any command, such as driving the pins of the dolphin insignia into the chest of the person who'd just passed the submarine qualifications to wear one. We wouldn't be doing that on the *Texas*. It violated the navy code and our commitment to treat one another with respect and dignity. Hazing incidents have caused ships to lose sailors. I simply would not let my family down or allow them to be jeopardized in that way.

My rule about respecting others was non-negotiable, and I only had to address this on a few occasions. Once, I witnessed a young officer strike a sailor in the groin as a joke. I was livid. I called the officer who'd given the "ball strike" into my stateroom for a pointed discussion on his behavior and how it worked against the culture of trust we were trying to create.

Immediately following the incident, I again brought the crew together topside. I related what had happened and asked for their help in preventing hazing in the future.

THINGS THAT MATTER

Showing love for the crew manifested in many ways. A master chief petty officer assigned to the *Texas* was set to retire after thirty years of service. Unfortunately, his retirement ceremony had been scheduled during an underway that was a critical Arctic certification workup. The crew respected the master chief petty officer and wanted to attend his retirement celebration. In my mind, the opportunity to go to the ceremony and honor a valued colleague did more for morale and a readiness mindset than a couple more days at sea would have.

I met with the commodore, "Sir, I intend to bring the ship in early so the crew can attend the master chief's retirement ceremony. They respect him and want to be there for him. It will do wonders for morale."

He looked at me like I had two heads.

I didn't blame him. We both recognized the tight constraints we were under and the importance of our time at sea. Certification for our mission was at stake, and time was not on our side.

"Do you trust me to have this crew ready ahead of schedule?" I asked.

He nodded.

"Let me pull the ship in for this man's ceremony," I requested. "He's part of our family."

The commodore gave his approval with significant reservations.

The sailors, however, were thrilled and expressed their appreciation. They'd seen that what mattered to them mattered to me, and they knew I would go to bat for them.

Changing the culture on our submarine took consistency and dedication. I continued to call on all the best practices I'd witnessed of my former leaders. I also tried to exhibit the sacrificial love my dad taught me. Trust, appreciation, the golden rule—these would all continue to turn the tide of the *Texas*.

—CHAPTER 15—

WHERE THE MAGIC HAPPENS

"Your gifts are not about you. Leadership is not about you. Your purpose is not about you. A life of significance is about serving those who need your gifts, your leadership, your purpose."

—Kevin Hall

Once trust was established and the crew knew my intentions were pure, the change was dramatic. Did I achieve 100 percent buy-in from the crew? Unfortunately, no. A few crew members just didn't have the right attitude. Like rowers in a boat, the men who had bought into the culture change were in front, passionately rowing and moving us forward. The ones who weren't sure were sitting in the middle with their oars out of the water, waiting to see where we were headed. And those in the back of the boat with their oars dragging were the ones attempting to stop the change.

The truth was, if they weren't going to paddle, we didn't need them in the boat. We reassigned these sailors or advanced their rotation dates to duties that aligned with their strengths and needs. I couldn't allow anything to impede our culture change when so much was at stake. The number of bad events seemed to correlate with the number of people in the back of the boat working against us. But once everyone began rowing together, we became unstoppable.

The crew of the USS *Texas* (official US Navy photo)

CHEERS!

At last, the day came to begin the cruise that would take us beneath the polar ice cap and to our new home port. As we departed Groton, Connecticut, and cruised through the Denmark Strait between Greenland and Iceland, I was filled with confidence. I observed an improved performance among the crew. The culture change we'd worked so hard on wasn't theoretical or Pollyannaish. While our mission to certify the Virginia-class for Arctic operations hadn't changed, the crew now engaged this mission with purpose. The correction in culture treated the root problem of apathy and reduced the opportunities for small and large deficiencies.

Fortunately, our crew performed impeccably well under the polar ice cap. Once underway, we maintained a constant state of readiness while maneuvering beneath and around icebergs. We needed to run some tests for Arctic certification, such as operating the emergency diesel generator and conducting the surfacing evolution. We looked for ice thin enough for us to break through to the surface but thick enough for a walkabout and an overnight stay. A chance to leave the sub would be great for crew morale.

The procedure went off without a hitch, but those few moments before giving the order to break through the ice were some of the tensest I have ever experienced.

Once completed, our crew climbed out of the sub and enjoyed a game of football. I had the opportunity to call our ship's sponsor, Laura Bush, on a satellite cell phone. I also phoned my family to check on my seven-year-old daughter, who had undergone eye surgery and been given anesthesia for the first time. The only communications we'd had while under the ice were the coded trigraph messages we received every fifteen minutes. Such a message might simply read, "ABC," meaning "everything is good, continue with operations," or "DEF," meaning "establish voice communication immediately."

I knew in the planning phase of the mission that we'd be ready for a celebration by the time we'd completed the surfacing procedure. I decided to bring beer for the occasion, although the squadron inspection team may have frowned on it. The funds in my credibility bank account with the squadron were pretty low at that point, and the beer issue could have been the straw that broke the camel's back. But I wasn't ignoring any rules; malt beverages are permitted on naval vessels for crews to enjoy at remote ports outside of the continental United States. And there was no denying the North Pole was remote!

We put guidelines in place to ensure the safety of the crew and ship. Each sailor over the age of twenty-one was allotted two beers but could not drink within eight hours of going on duty. Since we were there for two days, anyone who wanted could participate without having it impact their work. If there had been a negative incident, it would have affected my reputation, but I was willing to take that risk in order to reward them and let them know that I cared about them.

I told the crew, "You don't get paid enough for the hours you work and the sacrifices you make. How many people can say that they had a beer with their buddies in the Arctic Circle? Priceless. This is a small gift to you. Cheers!" The beer cans clanked as the men grinned and savored the experience.

I am sure someone is going to read this and gasp. I don't care. Seeing the smiles on their faces and the positive effect it had on morale made the reward worth the risk.

The ice continued to thicken so rapidly that it became impossible to continue to Pearl Harbor from the north. We were redirected to double back and navigate through the Panama Canal. This added more than a month to our transit time. It was a tough pill to swallow for the crew and our waiting families. The significant increase in sea time would have broken a crew with a poor culture. Fortunately, we had done the hard work and were ready to undertake the new challenge, despite our disappointment. We arrived safely in our new home port in late November of 2009.

EXPECTATIONS AND STANDARDS

Leadership affords the opportunity to form something special. Upon arriving in Pearl Harbor, I was still a new CO, but we had begun to create a great culture. I believed in the famous line adapted from the 1989 movie *Field of Dreams*: "If you build it, they will come." And they did! Soon, other sailors and officers were fighting to join the amazing team of individuals on the *Texas*. It wasn't all rainbows and sunshine, of course. Our team faced challenges, but the legendary culture we were building propelled us through difficult times.

Generally, a submarine captain begins as a junior officer, then becomes a department head, followed by XO, before finally becoming the CO. If they are fortunate, they might serve with a crew that earns one Battle "E." Two, at most. For a Battle "E" assessment, a crew must endure multiple rigorous inspections in all departments. Graders look at retention, battle readiness, and a host of other elements. Though I had served under some of the worst commands, I'd also served under four of the best. Already, I had been lucky enough to experience winning the Battle "E" four times. I knew how to build a crew that could win a Battle "E," and I was determined to get us there.

I didn't care about the personal glory of winning the competition, but I knew if we were the best, it would help our crew earn ribbons, promotions, rates, and reputational credit when sitting for a Fleet Sailor of the Year board. Plus, I knew the pride it would give my crew was invaluable payback for their stellar work. A mantra I learned under Grooms aboard the *Asheville* was "good guys get good deals." My crew was full of good and competent guys, and nothing would give me greater joy than to see their sacrifices and contributions rewarded with good deals.

We were charged with the operation of a cutting-edge nuclear submarine capable of running over thirty-three years without refueling. The entire fleet was watching our progress. More than just to win the Battle "E," we needed to uphold standards far beyond those of a typical ship in order to live up to the responsibility we'd been given.

Being upfront about expectations is critical to achieving best-in-class performance. And, as odd as this may sound, clear expectations and explanations of the purpose behind standards are a sign of love. Nothing says "I don't care about you" more than punishing someone for something they had no idea was wrong.

It was necessary for me to plainly define and routinely refer to specific standards. I had to ensure that these standards were met through monitoring and systems of accountability. The chance of a catastrophic event is directly proportional to the number of smaller-order deficiencies. If we had a major event that hurt even one of my crew members, then I wouldn't be living up to my promise to take care of my men personally and professionally. I had to reduce those chances for casualties by making sure no one in my crew was ignorant of those standards.

Since every crewmember had been required to read and acknowledge my written command philosophy, they understood foundational concepts such as "personal excellence leads to success" and "training breeds confidence." They had little excuse for violating one of these principles.

As I preached trust, standards, and purpose to my team, I began to realize these three elements composed the secret to building a legendary culture. The TSP Model (discussed in Chapter 20) delves further into these factors and offers a visual representation of their connectedness.

SQUARE PEGS

There were times we had "square pegs" on our crew who often wouldn't be treated well by the others. Square pegs were those who sincerely wanted to serve but just didn't have the same capabilities. Or, they had socially awkward personalities that alienated them from others. For one reason or another, square pegs didn't quite fit in like the rest and were perceived to have fallen short in some way. When a group of high-achieving individuals felt a square peg was impeding their success, they were generally quick to point out the sailor's flaws.

While I was on the *Asheville*, we had a second-chance sailor who had been kicked off another submarine for underperforming. He had been bullied on his previous ship because of his slow pace. Grooms recognized this right away, and he put his foot down with the first inkling of any unkindness. The sailor flourished once he was made part of the family.

Like Grooms, I simply would not tolerate any bullying behavior on the *Texas*. One of our square pegs was a junior officer I'll call Alfred. Alfred had a difficult time fitting in, and he didn't inspire the confidence of the crew. When I noticed that the men's initial lighthearted ribbing had turned mean, I gathered the other officers together in the wardroom to tell them that they needed to help Alfred along. If he failed to qualify as a watch stander, they would have to pick up the slack, so hindering his growth was not helping anyone. The officers agreed and rallied to help him prepare.

Alfred's defining moment on board came when he was scheduled to stand his first duty as a qualified ship's duty officer while the ship was in port. If he was allowed to single the duty, he would be the only officer on board after working hours. That was a big deal, particularly as the weather forecast showed an impending storm.

The predicted thunderstorm was an anomaly for Hawaii. We were hooked up to shore power, our diesel generator was under maintenance, and we were in the process of replacing our battery. If shore power went out, we could only rely on an auxiliary generator in which I had little confidence. If the power went out for an extended period, we could have safety issues with the reactor.

Under normal circumstances, I allowed my officers to decide if they were going to single the duty. If the workload was light, only one officer needed to be there. Carlos Martinez, the engineer, shared the responsibilities of the engineering duty officer that day with our newly qualified JO. Carlos called me around 6:00 p.m. and informed me that the JO was eager to single the duty for his first time.

"Do you think Alfred can handle it?" I asked.

"I think so," Carlos replied. "We walked through the procedure to bring the generator online. He understands the sequence."

Honestly, we both had concerns, especially considering the impending storm. But I knew if Alfred made it through the evening successfully, the dividends for him and the ship would be tremendous.

I told Carlos that he deserved to go home and be with his family that night, but that he needed to sleep with his cell phone by his ear and plan to leave for the ship at a moment's notice if there was a problem. Carlos agreed, so I allowed Alfred to take control. It was a risk. If something went wrong, I would be blamed, and my judgment would be questioned. But I was willing to take that chance.

Later, Alfred called me directly. The JO was eager to prove himself, just as I had been as an ensign. He wanted the responsibility of singling the duty. I asked him what his plan was if we lost shore power because of the storm. His strategy appeared sound, so I reiterated my permission for him to single the duty. I needed to give him the freedom to succeed or fail and learn from the experience.

To his credit, Alfred rose to the challenge and passed with flying colors. I told the whole crew, and we celebrated his achievement. It bolstered the team's confidence in the JO and the JO's confidence in himself. Alfred was no longer seen as a square peg, and his transformation was a testament to the positive influence of a trusting, family-like support system.

THE OPPORTUNITY OF A LIFETIME

During my last deployment as the CO, Gary Montalvo received the opportunity of a lifetime. If you recall from the introduction, Gary was the XO who'd said, "Let's see if we're pregnant," when we thought we'd been counter-detected.

He had been nominated to interview as a military aide to the president—the same role I had held. Ever dependent on the changing schedule of the commander in chief, the White House staff had to move the date of the interview. Unfortunately, the new date conflicted with a period when the *Texas* was scheduled to be at sea.

Gary was an excellent candidate, and I knew how important this opportunity was to him. I wanted this position for him as well. He was family, and I was going to do everything I could to make it happen. I contacted my leader to ask permission to excuse my XO from part of the transit to our next mission, and I received a half-hearted "okay." It was the kind of answer that I knew would likely change.

I then called the White House Military Office. If the interviews could be conducted in two days instead of three, we could make it work. Gary could catch a small boat transfer at the next port.

I explained to my squadron that the short underway period without my XO would allow my engineer, Carlos Martinez, to act as the executive officer and practice his skills until Gary's return. My immediate leadership was worried about our brief time at sea without Gary, but I knew that because of our excellent culture, we were up to the task. Despite squadron's concern, their okay was still active, so I took the opportunity to get my XO to the interview. I knew it was the right thing to do. As I drove Gary to the airport, I told him to turn off his cell phone until he landed in Washington, DC. Fingers crossed!

Sure enough, an hour after leaving Gary at the airport, I received a call ordering my XO *not* to go to Washington. I told them he was already gone, and I wasn't sure I could get a hold of him.

Gary made it to DC and was able to experience the White House interview process. He became the runner-up for the naval military aide position. Though the interviewers ultimately went in a different direction, Gary knew his whole work family supported him and had done all they could to be there for him. He'd gotten the chance to interview, so he wasn't left with the bitterness a missed opportunity can leave in its wake.

Including the *Texas*, Gary served on three Battle "E"–winning crews. He went on to hold many positions in the navy, such as Naval Reactors and program analyst at the Office of the Secretary of Defense, in addition to winning the Vice Admiral James Bond Stockdale Award for Inspirational Leadership.[26]

From 2014 through 2017, Gary captained the USS *North Carolina* and received the Legion of Merit Medal for "exceptionally meritorious conduct" in his role as CO.[27] Like Grooms, Gary's respect and love for his crew drove his success. Shortly after leaving the *North Carolina*, he reflected on his time with his "Tarheels":

> My Tarheels challenged me on a daily basis, putting me to the test. I will forever be indebted to them for aggressively correcting me each and every time I fell short and always understanding that disagreement did not mean disrespect.
>
> Their backup, pushback and emotion energized me and kept the Tarheel boat pointed straight ... they showed me the definition of teamwork ...
>
> I have been blessed with many mentors in life, but my Tarheels as a collective were my best mentor yet. I was truly blessed with the true joy of having courtside seats to their success. They made me a better CO and in the end a better person.[28]

These are the words of a servant leader. Gary continues to be a rising star in the submarine force and, at the time of this writing, commands Submarine Squadron Development FIVE. He is also my close friend.

BATTLING FOR THE BATTLE "E"

A squadron representative was riding with us during our operational reactor safeguard exam (ORSE) when he leaked to my second COB, Master Chief Matt Harris, that the decision for the recipient of that year's Battle "E" had already been made, and it wasn't us. When Matt relayed this to me, it was like a gut punch. My crew had worked so hard and done so well; I couldn't see why we were being passed over.

At the time of the commodore's decision, our ORSE had not been completed, and he had not been briefed on the totality of our deployment. I couldn't stand the injustice of his decision being made with an incomplete picture. As it turned out, we scored *very* well on the ORSE; in fact, we scored the best possible grade. We also achieved top marks on our tactical readiness exam (TRE) and inspections—supply, medical, etc.—across the board. Our attrition rate was low, and retention and promotion rates were high. On top of all that, we'd just finished a deployment. I didn't see how we could have done better. My men deserved the Battle "E," and I was willing to fracture my relationship with the commodore to fight for it, just as Grooms had fought for the crew of the *Asheville* when he disagreed with the ORSE results.

I don't believe my objections were well received, but when faced with the facts, the commodore relented and awarded my crew the Battle "E." The team deserved it for their hard work and the way they cared for the ship. Recognition for my crew was a cause worth fighting for.

LIKE CLOCKWORK

When I started my journey on the USS *Texas* and instituted the Crew Top Three, the number of concerns seemed endless and their severity felt overwhelming. Toward the end of my assignment, the crew's greatest worries came down to the type of beverages served and the limited variety of hot sauces available on the mess decks. Hot sauce! At that point, I knew we had tamed our troubles and created the magical culture I'd been after.

The way we now began our final underway periods was euphoric compared to the way it had started. The confusion and chaos that once surrounded me had been replaced with the smooth functioning of a well-oiled machine. As I reached my parking spot the morning of the underway (not having had to sleep on the ship the night before), I could see the crane ready to pull the brow away from the submarine once I had crossed the walkway. The entire crew was on board, and the ship was ready.

Ding! *Ding*! *Ding*! *Ding*! "*Texas*, arriving." *Ding*! *Ding*! *Ding*! *Ding*! The signal indicating the captain's presence rang out as I walked on board.

My XO handed me a cigar from my humidor and said, "Captain, the ship is ready to get underway."

"Very well, XO," I said.

I made my way to the bridge, climbing the narrow, thirty-foot ladder outside my stateroom.

The officer of the deck said, "Good morning, Captain. Request to get the ship underway and single all lines."

With a smile, I answered, "Very well, get the ship underway and single all lines."

I lit my cigar and relished the precision of my team. It was like watching a V of birds flying together in unison, or seeing the Blue Angels perform a flawless show. It was a thing of beauty.

GOODBYE, *TEXAS*

After nearly three years of captaining the *Texas*, it was time to hand over control to the next CO. At my change-of-command ceremony, I had the opportunity to thank so many, including the ship's sponsor, Laura Bush, who was in attendance. She had done so many small gestures for our ship through the years, and I was deeply honored by her presence.

Change of Command ceremony when I left USS *Texas*. From left to right: Cmdr. Robert Roncska, RADM Bruce Grooms, and First Lady Laura Bush

I then had the privilege to tell everyone what an influence Bruce Grooms had been to me. I looked at the crew and gestured toward Grooms. "I want you to know that you have Admiral Groom's fingerprints all over you. You didn't know it then. But now you do."

I proudly spoke of our team's accomplishments, including having the lowest attrition and highest retention rates in the Pacific Fleet for two consecutive years. Other commanding officers called me afterward to learn what secret sauce I'd used to get those results. I told them I'd simply shown my crew that I cared about them, personally and professionally. I worked to build trust, provide purpose, and set expectations. A magical family culture developed naturally from those efforts, and as a result, nobody *wanted* to leave.

At the ceremony, I continued to reflect on my experiences. "Words truly cannot describe what it was like to be part of this awesome *Texas* family. Clearly, *Texas* achieved some amazing feats while I was in command," I said with a grin, "but years from now, when I'm in my rocking chair, I am not going to reminisce about these accomplishments and the impact we had on our national security. What I will think about are the personal experiences we shared and lifelong friends I have made." For me, it will always come down to family.

At the end of my ceremony, I walked off the *Texas* and reached over and touched the sail of the ship for the last time. I reflected on the distance we'd come in the last three years. I thought about how much I loved my team and how showing them they were loved made all the difference in the world. In that moment, I felt very proud—but also very exhausted.

—CHAPTER 16—

BUILDING LEADERS

"Effective leaders are made, not born. They learn from trial and error, and from experience."

—COLIN POWELL

After leaving the *Texas*, I was ready for a new challenge. I felt energized and eager to share the leadership lessons I'd learned with future submarine officers. My next assignment was as a prospective commanding officer instructor (PCOI).

The number of available positions dwindles as one climbs the ranks, so I was excited to be given a role that I felt would make a positive difference.

Though the new job was great, it would be another difficult one for my family. As a PCOI, I'd split my time between Pearl Harbor, Hawaii, and Groton, Connecticut. About four months out of the year, I would be on the East Coast, away from my family—in addition to the time I would spend at sea with my students. However, I felt called to teach the principles of leadership I'd learned under Grooms, Bush, and others, and had practiced myself on the *Texas*. It was critically important for officers to understand that high standards are an outgrowth of trusting, caring relationships. I wanted to teach techniques for building healthy, high-performing work families and show how to lead with love.

PCO SCHOOL

As a PCOI, my role was to prepare future executive and commanding officers for their tours. Following World War II, the navy realized that there were too many submarine captains who lacked the rigorous training necessary to perform in high-stress situations. To remedy this deficit, a course was designed to simulate intense wartime scenarios under extreme conditions, much like the training for navy SEALs and TOPGUN pilots.

Later, the submarine force decided to include future executive officers as well. Prior to my time on the *La Jolla*, I had been privileged to be one of three executive officers to attend the inaugural XO training, so I knew the course well. Students sat through three weeks of in-port training and exams to prove their technical and tactical expertise. Then, they advanced to an eighteen-day underway period of intense, back-to-back drills, with little to no sleep. A six-day debriefing period rounded out the course as students critiqued the actions of their classmates and received their classmates' feedback in return. It was a rigorous curriculum.

During the wartime exercises, the prospective commander in training took over one of three operational submarines that were selected from the fleet to participate in the course on a rotating basis. The PCO class divided students among the three submarines, and they went head-to-head during exercises. Each prospective commanding or executive officer took temporary command of a crew that was foreign to the PCO and had to complete the exercises with virtual strangers. The PCO instructors were on board as well, observing the planning, decision-making, and execution of the missions.

The PCO training included an instrumented range with designated targets. The training scenario might ask PCOs to navigate to a target and decommission it with tomahawk missiles and torpedoes, all while being chased from above and below. Their performance was measured based on their planning, active decision-making, operational excellence, and ability to respond under unexpected and compounding pressures. Each exercise increased in complexity, and there was never enough time between drills for a full night's sleep.

REMEMBERING MY TRAINING

I remember my time as an XO student like it was yesterday, and one scenario stands out from the others. The day started with a prospective CO on my submarine losing a head-to-head battle by making a rookie mistake that was almost laughable. His evasion tactic was to navigate in circles to avoid an exercise torpedo that was in the water searching for him. He hadn't considered his *own* torpedo after he launched it at the other ship. A wire connects a torpedo to the launching ship, allowing for communication between the ship and the weapon. The PCO's circular maneuvering caused the wire to get caught in the submarine's screw (propeller).

I was excited for my turn at the helm and the opportunity to play cat and mouse against another submarine. I didn't know the acting captain of the opposing submarine, but I found out later he was a prospective CO and the class leader. He was quiet, confident, and a little bit cocky.

When I took control, I had no idea the torpedo wire was wrapped around our screw from the previous exercise. Overhead, a small civilian fishing craft entered our training range.

"Red range, red range," echoed throughout the control room. The hydrophone—an underwater speaker used to broadcast messages from the range coordinator, who is located on land—notified us of a pause to our war game. We were required to wait for the fishing boat to pass before continuing. I tried to place the ship in an optimal position, giving us the best tactical advantage. However, my adversary was on my tail. With each maneuver, he stayed in close proximity. He mirrored my moves, keeping me in his sights as we waited for the "all clear" signal. I continued my maneuvers, and he kept copying my every action. It didn't make sense. After three maneuvers, I was exasperated. I turned to the PCOI on board.

"Captain, something is wrong. Every time I maneuver, this guy is on my ass. He's in my baffles, and I can't shake him. I must have a sound vulnerability."

I turned again, to prove my point. My opponent followed me.

"You're the captain in this scenario. Figure it out," the PCOI replied.

Then it dawned on me. I realized the torpedo wire must have become entangled in the screw, and the amplified noise threw our silent stealth out the window.

Game on. I was all in.

"Ahead full."

My opponent and I had the same tactical training, so if I wanted to outsmart him, I'd need to get creative. I remembered *The Hunt for Red October*, the movie that had made me want to join the submarine force, and I felt inspired to replicate a key maneuver in the film. We picked up speed to create a large gap. I wanted to get far enough ahead of my opponent to turn around and head right back at him, closing the distance before his weapon could enable.

Five minutes later, our speed created the space I needed. Instinctively, my head tilted up, and my eyes shifted overhead as the announcement rang throughout the corridors: "Green range, green range." The war games recommenced.

I was painfully aware that my adversary would launch a torpedo within moments. If I didn't change the current situation, our chance of survival was zero.

At the signal to begin, I made my planned 180-degree turn directly toward the enemy ship.

"Helm, left hard rudder." I commanded.

Boom!

I knew that sound broadcasted on the hydrophone was the separation of my wire, meaning my ship was back in full stealth mode. Silence now cloaked us as we headed directly toward the opposing submarine. I hoped he wouldn't detect my maneuver, and if he didn't, he would think I was still driving away from him. With luck, I was confounding the read on my opponent's equipment.

"Torpedo in the water! Torpedo in the water!" the sonar supervisor announced. "Bearing right in front of us."

We could hear the high-pitched motor of a torpedo going underneath us. Before the enemy weapon had time to enable, it sailed right past our ship. My tactic had succeeded, just like the movie! My opponent hadn't realized that I was facing him and moving straight toward his vessel, closing the gap. He'd miscalculated our distance.

As I got close to where I thought the enemy was, I ordered, "All back full."

"What?" asked the PCOI on board, in shock. He took a step toward me and gave me a confused look. He knew that my command would cause the ship to cavitate, and the resulting noise would give away our position.

I gave the instructor a look and held up my hand.

I thought, *You didn't offer your guidance when I asked for it. I am sure not going to accept it now.*

He raised his eyebrows, nodded, and stepped back, giving me latitude.

"All back full!" I repeated, just like Captain Mancuso.

Those in the control room looked at me wide-eyed, obviously doubting my decision. After the circular antics of the acting CO before me, they were wary, but they all followed my command.

We could feel the entire ship shake and the waters around us rock. A moment later, I ordered, "All stop."

My move clearly confused the other ship. The disturbance must have sounded as if we had launched our torpedo. Our opponent began evasive maneuvers, which gave away his location in a spectacular fashion. The sub lit up our sonar screens like a Christmas tree.

"There he is!" I said. "Firing point procedures. Sierra two-three, tube two." When we were ready, I gave the order to fire.

Not long after, the range coordinator announced, "Bullseye! Bullseye! Bullseye!"

We'd done it! I felt like Captain James T. Kirk changing the conditions for the Kobayashi Maru and beating the "no-win" scenario. It was a fun memory to have and the type of experience I'd now get to oversee for the next generation of submarine leaders.

PERFORMANCE VARIANCE

Being a PCO instructor was a unique job. It was one of the few billets that required rides on multiple submarines from numerous ports and of all classes, including diesel boats from the Australian navy. Stepping onto so many subs helped me see the degree of variability within the submarine fleet. Some ships had highly successful performance records, while others were lagging in exam outcomes, safety protocols, and mission success. The struggling ships actually provided the best learning environment for the PCOs. Navigating extreme exercises with a low-performing crew increased the challenge of the test scenarios and set the stage for real situations that many commanders would face with their own crews.

The variance in execution puzzled me since each ship in the fleet had similar technical and tactical ratings. I wanted to understand how highly standardized military operations led by a normalized pool of officers could result in such variation. I set out to find a root cause and quickly recognized the patterns of the underperforming crews.

Visual cues were my first indication. I thought back to what Grooms had taught me when he pulled me aside to view a neighboring ship in port. The sub had mooring lines that were drooping so badly they were in the water, its banner was hung on the brow with missing tie wraps causing it to flap in the wind, and there was a pile of discarded cigarette butts next to the brow's entrance. It was well known on the waterfront that this ship was suffering. The lack of pride in its appearance was clear evidence. Back in the day, submariners wore ball caps with the ship's insignia on them. If we saw sailors with that ship's insignia on their hats, we immediately felt sorry for them.

Standards for cleanliness and order are drilled into every sailor during basic training. Yet, 100 percent of the underperforming ships I entered showed a lack of pride in their appearance. Inattention to details was evident. Lines were not taut, surfaces were dusty, small bits of trash were in corners, placards were askew, banners sagged, and equipment was unpolished and often malfunctioning. There were larger issues as well. Water space management practices were deficient, standards were loose, and routine training and maintenance were incomplete.

A STRUGGLING SEAWOLF

During one training session, I embarked on a Seawolf-class submarine, one of the newest and most elite classes in the fleet. I found that just one of the three high-pressure air compressors was operable. The only functioning compressor was running continuously, in a reduced status, and couldn't keep up with the air demands of the ship. Multiple operations on a submarine rely on these air compressors, such as diving, surfacing, hydraulics, weapons discharge, and engine propulsion. Without sufficient air pressure in the air banks, all of these functions had the potential to fail. The ship would be unable to submerge, surface, sail, or strike. It would mean the loss of a mission, or worse yet, the loss of the ship and the crew.

I questioned the engineering section, and they told me they were aware of the situation. But there seemed to be a lack of ownership and no urgency to rectify the problem. The engineering department should have been relentless in fixing the compressors. Each successive layer of leadership should have been aware and actively working to resolve this problem. It concerned me that I was the only one pushing for a solution. Their lack of focus in overcoming such a critical issue showed me that the crew's apathy and the resulting breakdown in structure hadn't happened overnight. I wondered how they had gotten to that point and what else was being overlooked.

I paused training and called a meeting. I made it clear that the compressors needed attention before we could continue. We weren't in a training center; this was a real underway in a real submarine. Continuing under these conditions would put our lives at stake.

I began directing action and assigning accountability to the crew. We managed to return one compressor to full operational capacity and order the parts required to fix the remaining one. I couldn't understand why the captain or the engineer wasn't directing this; they had been living with the broken air compressors for weeks. Directing the repairs wasn't my responsibility. We resumed operations but continued to find small-order deficiencies. I knew I had to look to the crew for answers.

Crews often develop deep friendships as a result of long periods of confinement, working together and attempting to create a semblance of a normal life. Ideally, crews become a sort of brotherhood. The way they interact usually demonstrates their camaraderie to any visitor on board.

That was not the case here. Even before we set sail, I noticed a quiet on the ship. Laughter and good-natured ribbing were missing. I was seldom met in the halls with a smile or nod, much less a friendly "hello." Instead, I passed bent heads and averted gazes. The team was flat, and something was clearly amiss. It was time to solicit input from the sailors.

MISSING MICKEY

Whenever I was aboard a submarine, I tried to build a rapport with the crew. I would interact with the sailors to get to know them and understand how I could support them. I started my own informal Crew Top Three on the struggling Seawolf and found that many sailors and officers were aching for a more positive culture. They craved community and a shared purpose. They wanted to be supported and feel valued.

One officer told me, "I just wanted to see Mickey Mouse."

I was confused. "What do you mean, shipmate?"

He explained his disappointment. Stationed in Bremerton, Washington, his ship had been nearing the end of an extended overhaul period in the shipyard. To be recertified, the ship had to pass all portions of an inspection, including a cleanliness and preservation section. Two weeks before the scheduled inspection, the COB, with the captain's permission, directed all crew members to come in seven days a week to concentrate on the deep cleaning that needed to be done. Unfortunately, the inspection got postponed about two and a half months due to equipment failure. But instead of telling the crew they could go back to a regular cleaning routine until the new date for the inspection, the COB maintained the rigorous schedule. For three months, the crew worked seven days a week, polishing the same nooks and crannies over and over again.

After the inspection, the submarine left for Pearl Harbor to participate in our submarine command course. There was a stop planned in San Diego along the way that was meant to be part preparation for the PCO course and part liberty. When the young officer learned about the planned port of call, he set his heart on going to Disneyland and seeing Mickey Mouse. Unfortunately, he never got the chance to go. All the officers were restricted to San Diego and ordered to run attack-center simulations the entire time they were in port.

The missed opportunity broke the young officer's spirit and diminished his desire to serve. His captain had no compassion for his crew and treated them like they were just commodities. It was no wonder his crew stopped caring for the ship.

There's an old joke that compares leaders to a tree full of monkeys. The monkeys on the top limbs look down and see smiling faces. The monkeys at the bottom of the tree look up and see nothing but asses.

The prolonged work hours and the excessive cleaning that occurred in this situation might have impressed the monkeys at the top of the tree when the submarine was finally inspected, but the overworked monkeys on the bottom branches certainly had a different view.

INSTILLING STANDARDS

As I continued to serve as an instructor, more stories like the young officer's surfaced. I discovered that the captains of underperforming ships had other similarities in their leadership styles besides their lack of compassion. They rarely interacted with their team, professionally or personally. They also resorted to captain's masts as a form of discipline far more frequently than the average command, just as my predecessor on the *Texas* had. The poor culture found in each underperforming ship was clearly the root cause of their struggle. It was a direct result of captains who failed to lead with love.

My theories about the link between performance and culture had solidified by this point. Within five minutes of walking on board a new submarine, my gut would tell me whether it was a good or bad ship—and my gut was shockingly accurate. It was less about what was done and more about *how* it was done.

Though cultural transformation takes a concerted effort over time, I did what I could to coach the executive and commanding officers while on board. During debriefings, we discussed their observations and mine. I taught them to notice concerning behaviors of the crew and how to use their influence to amend those behaviors. I tried to show each prospective commander how serving the crew had both professional and personal implications. I hoped to instill the desire to create an atmosphere of trust, purpose, standards, and love.

— CHAPTER 17 —

Fairwinds and Following Seas

"Great is the art of the beginning, but greater is the art of ending."
—Henry Wadsworth Longfellow

After my tour as a PCO instructor, I spent two years in Millington, Tennessee, a suburb of Memphis—the birthplace of rock-and-roll and home to the best barbecue I've ever eaten. While in Millington, I was a detailer for commanding and post-commanding officers. My role was to place people in positions that fit their talents, needs, and desires, while also fulfilling the requirements of the navy.

FEDEX AND FRED

Millington is also home to FedEx. One of the most interesting experiences I had in Millington was touring the FedEx facility. I was in awe of the organizational tempo. Thirty planes circled in the air, continuously landing and taking off. Like an Indy 500 pit crew, teams were poised to load cargo holds and refuel tanks the moment a plane touched down. Within minutes of landing, planes were backed out and taking off again. I could easily see how FedEx could uphold its brand promise of delivering a package "when it absolutely, positively has to be there overnight."[29]

Unlike FedEx deliveries, the company's success didn't happen overnight. When founder and CEO Fred Smith first wrote about his idea for next-day, small-package delivery service for an economics class assignment at Yale, he received a C on his paper.[30] He went ahead with his idea anyway. He had a rocky start and even turned to a blackjack table in a moment of desperation to keep the company afloat, but ultimately, Smith was able to realize his vision.[31]

Shortly after I visited the FedEx facility, I learned that Smith was coming to tour our base. Each community of naval operations (surface warfare, aviation, submarines, etc.) were tasked with informing him about their specialty. I was chosen to be one of those who briefed Smith and was excited to meet the legendary business leader in person.

The surface warfare guy gave his spiel first, listing the numbers of ships, where they were deployed, and so on. When he finished his presentation, he asked Smith if he had any questions. We all assumed Smith would say something like "Thanks, great brief. Keep up the good work." Instead, he had a stern, almost upset look, and asked specifically about the littoral combat ship. He wanted to know about the significant building delays, operational shortfalls, and major cost overruns. None of us had been expecting this kind of scrutiny. An awkward quiet filled the room.

The aviation officer went next, and I hoped Smith would take it easier on him. He didn't. Smith questioned the aviation officer on the problems with the joint strike fighter.

It was my turn next. By then, my excitement had changed to anxiety. I started to sweat and thought, *What did I sign up for?* It must have been what the poor, unfortunate souls who'd been interviewed by Rickover had felt.

I braced myself, but before I opened my mouth to speak, Smith stood up, pointed his finger at me, and declared, "The submarine force. You guys! You guys are the reason we have not gone to war with China. You are the reason they have not invaded Taiwan. You are our modern-day heroes. The Virginia-class program is the gold standard for ship acquisition, and you guys are the cream of the crop for our country. I thank you for your service and how you prevent wars through your presence and deterrence."

I looked at the other two presenters, dumbfounded. I didn't expect Smith's response and felt sheepish being praised in the face of the criticism the others had received. Despite the good-natured ribbing between the naval communities and the branches of the armed services, we're all vital to the security of the nation.

However, at that point, I had lived in the submarine community for twenty-six years and had never run across any civilian who so clearly stated our reason and value. I appreciated the recognition for our often overlooked, silent service. Smith reinforced my sense of purpose, and I wanted to pay it forward. I often shared my interaction with Fred Smith with submarine officers. It was my way of reminding them of the "why" of their service, as well as their importance to our nation.

SQUADRON COMMAND

There were many positives to being a detailer. I made a difference, got an insider's view of detailing, and had an abundance of quality family time. However, I never really felt the same satisfaction I enjoyed when I was a hands-on leader. So when I received orders to return to Pearl Harbor as the commodore of Squadron Seven—the largest squadron with ten submarines—I was thrilled.

At squadron, I would have the chance to mentor commanding officers, certify submarines for operations, ensure ship and crew safety, and uphold national security. It was time to get back into the game again, and I was ready!

Immediately, I began to assess the cultures on the submarines in my squadron. There was no way I could micromanage ten submarines, so I utilized feedback from my top-notch staff and from any temporary rider who could give me an outsider's view. Chaplains gave me generalized reports about their monthly visits and requests for mental health counseling.

If I heard about a new crew member being forced to sleep on the mess decks or a submarine that didn't have the proper supplies, I took the news as a sign of poor culture. I set up metrics for determining when I should intervene. Once a threshold was exceeded, I acted immediately and scheduled face time with the commanding officer. I knew by now that where bad culture brewed, the propensity for accidents would surely follow.

PERSONNEL SHIFTS

Each squadron evaluates the readiness of its submarines for deployment with a Pre-Overseas Movement Certification (POM Cert). This certification tests the submarine's war-fighting skills and readiness. But long before the certification process, I usually had clear, serious indicators if a ship's culture was poor.

This was true of one particular ship in my squadron. To begin with, a breakdown in an elementary procedure had led to the destruction of a very costly piece of equipment. Each submarine has a towed array sonar or a series of hydrophones that trail behind the ship. If the towed array is in need of maintenance when in port, it is tied to the pier, as was the case with this submarine's array. But upon completion of its maintenance, it was never untied, and the ship tried to get underway with it still attached, completely destroying the multimillion-dollar piece of equipment. Such a blatant oversight was a major red flag, and frankly, mind-boggling. Every single crew member had to have walked past and seen the array still tied to the pier, but no one said a word. Additionally, required pre-underway checklists included ensuring that the sonar array was untied, so clearly, basic procedures weren't being followed. The expensive debacle revealed fault on so many levels.

Then, there was the treatment of the ship's CS specialist who was home on leave. He'd kicked off his vacation with a few adult beverages—not a lot, but too many for him to drive. The specialist received a phone call from the XO telling him to return to the ship because the CO wanted to speak to him.

"Sir, I am on leave," the CS specialist said. "I've had a few drinks and can't drive right now."

"Have your wife drive you," the XO answered.

"It's late, and my kids are in bed. She'd have to wake them and take them with us."

"That's fine," he said. "Have her do that."

With his wife as chauffer and groggy children in the backseat, the CS specialist arrived at the boat to be told by his captain, "You are terrible at your job, and you're a substandard submariner. Now go home."

The CO and XO were a nightmare pair. The CO had unreasonable ideas, and instead of being the voice of sanity, the XO did anything the CO wanted. They didn't balance each other out.

In the navy, we use the term missile-mission matching to ensure we're using the right missile for the target. The same is true with personnel. The right people have to be matched to the right ship and to each other. Prior to this command duo, the culture on this particular ship had been good. But with two authoritarian leaders in charge, the shell-shocked crew began to decline rapidly.

After much consideration, I decided to make an unprecedented move by changing this XO with an XO that had a reputation for leading with love. My decision was controversial and met with skepticism by my superiors, but I stood my ground.

Things improved some. The XO did provide a counterbalance to the CO. But the ship's problems weren't solved completely. The navigator was underperforming in a multitude of areas. It was his duty, for instance, to ensure the thirty or so crew members who would be privy to top-secret, mission-specific details acquired the proper security clearances before a six-month deployment. Even though the process took six to eight months to complete, and the ability to deploy rested on those clearances, the navigator had to be reminded many times to work on them.

Both the navigator's lack of action and his attitude were detrimental to the ship. When my deputy, Mike Majewski, was on board to prepare the submarine for the POM Cert, he heard the navigator being openly confrontational and defiant with the CO over the conn. In an attempt to mentor the navigator, Mike sat down with him and laid out a plan with caring standards. It was a strategy for improvement with clear measures of accountability. Mike was simple and direct, leaving no room for misinterpretation.

For the POM Cert, I took my turn at riding the submarine. During the initial brief, it was painfully obvious that the navigator's performance had not improved, and his defiant attitude was continuing to negatively impact the culture and safety of the ship. Something drastic had to change.

So, I made another unprecedented move. I canceled the POM Certification and ordered the captain to return to port as soon as possible. I told him, "I am not certifying your ship for deployment under the current circumstances."

The CO knew something should have been done about the navigator much earlier, but he had felt his hands were tied. He seemed both embarrassed and relieved by my order.

When the captain announced the ship would be returning to port immediately, shock waves swept through the crew. No one—including me—had ever heard of a POM Cert getting pulled like this. The navigator's openly belligerent attitude had gone unpunished for so long that the crew never expected there to be repercussions. The serious consequence they were finally witnessing was a clear indicator of coming change. It jump-started a shift in culture.

Already past his nominal rotation date, the navigator was relieved of his duty early (not technically fired), and the squadron's weapons officer, Daniel Futch, took over the role after earning his navigator's certification. At the time, Futch was enjoying shore duty with us, and it was hard to take him away from his family. However, he was a great leader with exceptional operational experience. What's more, he was ready and willing to row.

Though the double shift in leadership was unprecedented, it was essential to the mission and safety aboard the ship. With a noticeable change in culture that continued to improve with time, the team members went on to pass their recertification and complete their deployment successfully.

THE COMMODORE'S CUP

Not all cultural work is uncomfortable or difficult. Sometimes it's fun.

Back when I'd been a department head on the *Asheville*, the commodore of Squadron Three had organized an event he called "Commodore's Cup." At some point in the ten years that followed, the competition had become defunct. But I had fond memories of gathering once a year with the crews of Squadron Three to compete in games such as tug-of-war, three-legged races, and cribbage. It was a great way to build squadron camaraderie, and the winning submarine got to display a trophy on board for the following year.

I was anxious to recreate the Commodore's Cup, but I wanted to do it bigger. With the help of Morale, Welfare, and Recreation (MWR), we rented Aloha Stadium, home of the NFL's Pro Bowl. In addition to the original competitions, we added field-goal kicking and flag football. We also had barbeque. Saying the event went over big is putting it mildly.

Camaraderie was important within the submarine community. Boats with already-established relationships are more willing to help one another in a time of need. Not only did I want the Commodore's Cup to foster camaraderie, but I hoped to communicate my love and appreciation for my teams as well. I also wanted to inspire the submarine commanders to bring that same spirit of love and team building into their leadership practices.

ANOTHER FIELD OF DREAMS

As I had on the *Texas*, I set out to build a *Field of Dreams* environment at the squadron, and just like *Texas*, I attracted some of the best talent the navy had to offer—most notably, my deputy, Mike Majewski. Like me, Mike knew a mission would be successful if he put people first. He loved people and would go above and beyond to help others. He was a mentor and molder of future leaders. Mike was humble, but he looked and acted like Pixar's Mr. Incredible.

I joked with Mike on day one: "My goal is to sit here and eat Cheetos while you run this place." Although I don't actually eat Cheetos—at least, not often—I wanted to give Mike the latitude to make his own decisions. I trusted him and knew he would do great things.

Another talent to join our team was Joe Campbell, an engineering officer. Unfortunately for Joe, he had been in a shipyard environment without getting any sea time, which negatively impacted his chances for promotion. Joe's previous commodore in Bremerton, Jeff Jablon, asked that I bring Joe in as an operations officer. That was unheard of; operations officers were traditionally former navigators with abundant sea time. However, I didn't want to see Joe's potential go to waste. As a former operations officer, I knew the ins and outs of the role, and I could guide him. It was another person-first, "outside the box" gamble that paid off. Currently, Joe Campbell is the commander of one of our nation's most elite submarines.

A CAUTIONARY TALE

I love to teach by telling stories, both my own and those of others. To impress upon my officers the importance of upholding standards, especially safety standards, I would recount one of the most devastating stories in naval history: the sinking of the USS *Indianapolis*.

In July of 1945, the *Indianapolis* was ordered to transport a black canister with top-secret contents to Tinian Island in the Northern Marianas. Even the commanding officer, Captain Charles B. McVay III, had no idea what was inside the canister. We now know it was uranium and components for the atomic bombs that would later be dropped on Japan. After their mission was complete, the ship continued to Guam, where McVay received orders for the next part of their transit to Leyte, in the Philippines. McVay was told there would be no destroyer escort, but not to worry because there was minimal risk from enemy submarines. He was also told to zigzag as a precaution during the day and use his discretion at night. He was not informed that a periscope had been spotted in the area or that a destroyer had been sunk a week earlier. With a false sense of security, McVay decided not to zigzag at night.[32]

At 12:15, on the morning of July 30, the *Indianapolis* was torpedoed by a Japanese submarine. Within twelve minutes, the ship sank with approximately three hundred men still on board. The remaining 890 men, Captain McVay included, were stranded in the water with only a few lifeboats and almost no food or water. For four days, McVay was forced to listen to his crew's sounds of agony as they suffered from dehydration, exposure, hallucinations, and, most terrifying of all, shark attacks. Indeed, the sharks were so bad that their assault on the men of the *Indianapolis* is still the deadliest attack of its kind in recorded history. Only 316 men survived.[33]

The navy later court-martialed McVay for failure to zigzag at night and order abandon ship after they were hit. He was acquitted of the latter but convicted of the former. Though McVay obeyed the orders he'd been given, he didn't adhere to the wartime standard, which was to zigzag. Since he was without a destroyer escort, he should have had an especially heightened sense of caution.[34]

In time, the degree of McVay's culpability would be questioned. Japanese admiral Hashimoto, who had sunk the *Indianapolis*, testified that, because of his submarine's superior position, zigzagging wouldn't have saved the *Indianapolis*. Other American sub experts also testified that zigzagging would have given negligible advantage in eluding the enemy. Some felt McVay was used as a fall guy. Others thought Admiral Ernest King, who recommended the court martial, was acting on an old grudge. Fifty years after the incident, Captain McVay was posthumously exonerated of any wrongdoing.[35] The damage had been done, though, and McVay's life had been destroyed by the consequences.

In addition to the trauma of the event and the blame placed on his shoulders, McVay received hate mail for years afterwards, including a letter that stated, "Merry Christmas! Our family's holiday would be a lot merrier if you hadn't killed my son."[36]

He struggled with poor mental health, finally taking his own life at age seventy.

I imagine that McVay tortured himself, in part, because he hadn't followed procedure to the letter. Even if zigzagging wouldn't have changed the *Indianapolis*'s fate, no one—including McVay himself—could have blamed a captain who did everything by the book. *This* was what I wanted my officers to understand: maintaining standards was critical. It protected the ship and protected them.

When one feels invincible, as young leaders often do, it's easy to think policies and procedures aren't that vital. I always shared McVay's story before my COs deployed because I never wanted them to take shortcuts they might later doubt or regret. I loved them and didn't want them to suffer unintended consequences.

THE IMPACT OF EFFORT

My most rewarding experience as commodore didn't happen at sea, but from an interaction that impacted the personal life of a friend. During one of my morning runs, I passed a former *Texas* shipmate, Jared Mankins. It had been four years since I had last seen Jared, but we picked up just where we had left off. I asked him about his wife, Amber, and his current ship assignment. Jared hesitated a moment, then wanted to know if he could stop by my office to discuss his rotation. I told him to come over anytime.

When Jared came by, he presented me with his dilemma. He had orders to leave Hawaii, but he and Amber had been on a very long waiting list to start in vitro fertilization on Oahu. Jared's original orders had him leaving

Hawaii in October, after their appointment. However, his rotation date had recently been moved up by two months—before they were scheduled to start treatment. There was no commercial in vitro clinic that would accept their military insurance at the new duty station, and without the insurance, it would be over twenty thousand dollars extra per cycle—an impossible amount on a sailor's budget. He'd begged the detailer to allow them to stay in Hawaii a little longer.

The detailer had said to him, "Man, listen. They're called 'orders' for a reason. I knocked my wife up the first time we were together, so I don't understand what problems y'all are having, but figure it out in South Carolina."

Jared worked through his chain of command. He asked his engineer, his XO, his CO, and his commodore for help, but faced closed doors. The detailer told him to quit calling because "the orders weren't going to change."

Having been a detailer myself, I knew there were things that could have been done to accommodate Jared and his wife. I was infuriated and embarrassed that no one in leadership had put in the effort to make a difference. Jared was no longer in my chain of command, but I was anxious to help. I made a phone call and a non-negotiable order. Jared wasn't looking for a change of assignment; he just wanted his rotation moved back to the original date. This was a once-in-a-lifetime chance for him and his wife.

With minimal effort, we were able to move Jared's orders to fit the needed timeline. Helping out was the right thing to do, but it had been such a quick, easy task that I forgot about it until Jared called me the day that he and his wife were leaving the island. He told me the good news: Amber was pregnant! Months later, they welcomed a healthy baby into their family.

The experience taught me what a powerfully beneficial effect even small deeds can make. A two-minute phone call turned out to be one of the most impactful actions of my naval career. Every effort makes a difference!

A NECESSARY ENDING

During my time as commodore, my team and I successfully deployed eight submarines to the Western Pacific and guided numerous ships through extended maintenance periods. We also focused on rehabilitating struggling leaders. Most of them were willing to do the hard work necessary to regain their right to be in command. I was proud of my squadron COs, my team, and what we'd accomplished. But there were drawbacks to my role and career that became more apparent over time.

By the end of my tour, my daughter would be finishing her freshman year in high school. If I continued in the navy, she would likely be forced to change schools two more times before she graduated. We were tired of moving and tired of starting over. We wanted some stability for our children, and my wife wanted me at home.

I was at the stage in my career where my peers were thinking about screening for admiral. If I had continued, I don't know if I would have been selected; I don't think anyone in my situation ever knows for sure. But in twenty-eight years, I had gotten to know and observe many admirals. Not much about the job appealed to me, and not much of it appealed to my wife. Stephanie and I concluded that my current duty should be my last.

One night, while my wife and I were winding down after a full day, we took a long walk on Kailua beach, feeling the wet sand under our feet, listening to the waves, smelling the salty air, and recapping our days. After she filled me in on the third-grade hijinks happening in her classroom, I turned to her and said, "I put in my retirement papers today."

She knew it was coming; she just hadn't expected it so soon.

One thing had pushed me to do it that day. A friend, who I respected and loved, was in an assignment that he flat out didn't like. He dealt with it respectfully, as one does in such a position, but as his confidant, I was privy to his real dissatisfaction with the role.

That day, he called to tell me he'd just screened for admiral. I was excited for him. He deserved it, and he wanted it.

After sharing his news, my friend said, "Bob, you really should come to relieve me. This job would be great for you!"

He and I both knew what his current job entailed, and we both knew that it was not, in fact, "great." But it would give me visibility and the opportunity to advance. My friend was looking out for me and my career. There was just one problem: I was not interested in spending time in a role I wouldn't enjoy, hoping it would lead to my first admiral star. My priorities became crystal clear, and to meet those priorities, I needed to say farewell to the navy. I felt I had another calling, even if I wasn't sure at that moment what it was.

To borrow a term from Dr. Henry Cloud, one of my favorite authors, it was time for a "necessary ending."[37]

From left to right: Cmdr. Robert Roncska, Stephanie, Sophia, and Zack

PART FIVE:
LEADERSHIP BEYOND THE SEA

— CHAPTER 18 —

BEYOND THE SEA

"An incident is just the tip of the iceberg, a sign of a much larger problem below the surface."

—Don Brown

My choice to leave the navy caused some blowback. Admiral Grooms called to express his extreme disappointment. He said he had never been angrier with me. There was still work to be done to improve the life of sailors, and he wanted me to stick around and keep at it. But ultimately, Grooms said he understood that my family had to come first.

My decision was not typical for others in my position. In fact, it was almost unheard of. Most commodores stay and do more tours in the hopes of achieving the next rank of admiral.

Navy officers who do retire often go on to some form of government contracting. I put my feelers out in all directions and didn't discount some type of government work.

Stephanie and I made a list of places we would like to settle, and Orlando, Florida—where we'd lived when I was an instructor in Nuclear Power School—made the short list. We both loved the area and felt we could easily build a life there.

AN UNEXPECTED OFFER

Over the years, I'd kept in close contact with Dr. Jeffrey Kuhlman, the president's physician who'd stitched me up after my bike accident in Beijing. He had settled in the Orlando area and worked for a large healthcare system there. I called him and asked if he had any connections with local companies, such as Lockheed Martin, that he could introduce me to. His response perplexed me.

"Why don't you come work for the hospital?" he asked.

Given that I had absolutely no clinical experience or any inkling about how healthcare functioned, I had no idea what I would contribute. Jeff went on to tell me about David Bonacum. A former nuclear submarine junior officer, Bonacum began working in healthcare after his separation from the military. He made significant contributions to patient safety by leveraging his high-reliability training. Bonacum introduced the use of the Situation, Background, Assessment, and Recommendations (SBAR) communication tool to healthcare while working for Kaiser Permanente, and it became an industry standard for patient safety. Dr. Kuhlman continued, "You can bring your experience in high-reliability and leadership to the hospital and build on what he's done."

I was intrigued but skeptical. I found David Bonacum on LinkedIn and set up a phone call to gather more insight. When I called him at our prearranged time, I could hear crowds of people and a bell ringing in the background. I was concerned that it was a bad time to connect. "No," he assured me, "I teach high school now. I'm starting my break."

"High school?"

It turns out David had moved on from healthcare to teaching disadvantaged students. I was beyond impressed with him. He was a people-first leader. David told me that my submarine experience would translate well into healthcare, and he encouraged me to give it a try.

After a long interview process, the healthcare system offered me a newly created position: executive director for safety and high reliability. I would dedicate the next chapter of my life to ensuring that patients had the safest experience possible within a hospital setting. It would be a pivot away from the leadership roles I'd held in the navy, but the lessons I learned on leading with love and building a magical culture would certainly come into play.

RESEARCHING THE PROBLEM

Even to someone like me who had no background in healthcare, it was obvious that medicine was a high-stakes field. What I didn't realize at the time, though, was the amount of harm that preventable errors caused on a regular basis.

I began my role by researching medical mistakes, and what I discovered was chilling. Studies showed annual deaths in the US related to human error were on the rise, climbing from 98,000 to 250,000 per year![38] This statistic did not even account for the vast numbers of near misses or the patients who were maimed or suffered harm to a lesser degree because of simple mistakes. Indeed, many of the mistakes *were* simple: Failure to note blood type. Failure to verify patient identity. Failure to confirm which leg was to be amputated. Failure to double-check medicine type and dosage.

Researchers at Johns Hopkins found that most medical mistakes weren't caused by bad doctors or nurses per se—but rather by systemic issues such as poorly coordinated care and the underuse of safety nets.[39]

It wasn't that healthcare was devoid of safety protocols. There was, for instance, the Five Rights procedure, introduced by Dr. Jerome Osheroff in 2007 and well known to medical professionals. To follow the Five Rights process, a medical professional need only confirm that they had the right patient, the right drug, the right dose, the right route, and the right time.[40] These simple confirmations could prevent a world of harm. Despite this foundational protocol, mistakes that the Five Rights should have prevented continued to occur.

This was a clear indicator of "drift"—a casual departure from careful adherence to safety protocols over time. It was one of the issues I had witnessed on the struggling ships in the nuclear navy.

My intuition told me that the root cause of medical mistakes was a combination of human and system error, as well as a broader problem with culture. If I could translate my experience in the nuclear navy to patient safety, I could help improve outcomes and prevent major mistakes.

FOUR ISSUES TO ADDRESS

As I familiarized myself with my new industry through questions, observations, and more research, I identified four critical differences between healthcare and the nuclear navy. In the nuclear navy, safety was proactive. Procedures were followed to prevent problems from occurring. In healthcare, however, most departments had grown so lean that proactive processes had slipped, and safety issues were handled with a reactionary, stopgap response.

Another difference between navy and healthcare involved transparency and the sharing of lessons learned. When a near miss happened in the navy, the incident was reported to the entire fleet so that others could learn from it. (Of course, there were cases like Captain Fenwick and our event in the Strait of Hormuz when this didn't occur, but this lack of transparency was rare.) In healthcare, information was siloed and "no harm, no foul" seemed to be the rule.

In the navy, a common adage is "don't be afraid to call the baby 'ugly,'" meaning one should address problems no matter how awkward it is to do so. I found my new colleagues reluctant to call the baby "ugly" for a number of reasons—fear of looking bad as a leader, fear of getting in trouble, or fear that doing so would divert resources needed elsewhere. These were all legitimate concerns, but ones that needed to be overcome for the greater good of patient safety.

Finally, I discovered a problem of sustainment in healthcare. Once an issue was identified and corrected, there should have been rechecks to make sure the resolution to the problem remained implemented and effective. In the nuclear navy, sustainability was maintained through a system of observations, questions, and training logs. In healthcare, staffing levels were lean, and personnel turnover was high. Staff members were so busy that drift from sustainment procedures occurred frequently.

These were the four areas I believed could offer the greatest potential for improvement in safety: reactive vs. proactive responses, transparency, willingness to speak up, and sustained follow-through.

CULTURE VARIABILITY

The nuclear navy and healthcare did share one workplace characteristic: the variation in cultures among departments. There were great leaders who valued their team members, brought out the best in them, and fostered a healthy culture of openness and accountability. Then, there were iron-fisted MFBs who deprived their teams of psychological safety and the confidence to speak up.

I could see the old toxin of apathy infiltrating those struggling cultures. Understaffing, supply chain issues, and a perceived lack of support led many to feel undervalued and to disengage from their work.

Most healthcare workers are inherently caring people who chose their field based on a desire to serve others. If these workers felt empowered and valued, I knew the apathy would disappear and outcomes would improve. I was confident that leading with love and using the high-reliability principles of the nuclear navy would transform culture, performance, and safety in healthcare. I was eager to get started!

— CHAPTER 19 —

Making a Difference

"I alone cannot change the world, but I can cast a stone across the water to create many ripples."

—Mother Teresa

Curled in the fetal position wearing nothing but an adult diaper, a frail man in his mid-twenties lay moaning and shaking on top of a bare twin bed. I peered at him through the window of his stark room in the psychiatric unit, disturbed by his state. Surely a better solution could be found!

I had been asked to assess this psych unit by the system's director of behavioral health who had been concerned by the department's safety record: three preventable deaths within six months' time. The scene before me didn't instill confidence.

I turned from the window to seek out the ward's psychiatrist and question him about the patient I'd observed. What I learned was astonishing. The psychiatrist told me the man didn't belong in a psych ward. "He doesn't have a mental health issue," the psychiatrist said. "He has Parkinson's."

It wasn't clear why the man with Parkinson's was unresponsive, but staff of the unit said, with evident resentment, that it was typical for the emergency department to send patients to the psych unit when they didn't know what else to do with them. Within the hour, I was speaking with the hospital's chief medical officer on the patient's behalf and was assured that the situation would be remedied immediately.

That evening, I received a call from the ward's psychiatrist. The Parkinson's patient had died. His blood sugar levels had been extremely low, and it was this hypoglycemia which had kept him from communicating.

The tragedy launched a full-scale investigation into the psychiatric unit and an overhaul of its principles and practices. The memory of the case has remained with me as a haunting reminder of what can happen when cultures turn toxic and standards fail in high-risk fields.

LAYING A FOUNDATION

I was given a team of highly qualified and passionate patient safety officers and nurses. With the team's clinical expertise, I was certain we could positively address the four trouble areas I'd identified using methods similar to those of Admiral Rickover. By laying a foundation of clear standards and structures of accountability, we could achieve consistent outcomes and enhance safety throughout the hospital system.

Anyone familiar with healthcare might think my team and I were trying to reinvent—or reintroduce—the wheel. After all, the Five Principles of High Reliability Organizations described by Karl Weick and Kathleen Sutcliffe in 2007 have been commonly adopted in healthcare: deference to expertise, reluctance to simplify, sensitivity to operations, commitment to resilience, and preoccupation with failure.[41]

Though Weick and Sutcliffe's principles are absolutely aligned with those of the nuclear navy, they aren't expressed in clear and precise language that is easy to understand or explain. As a result, the principles often go unapplied.

We wanted to follow in Admiral Rickover's shoes by keeping our principles simple.

DISNEY'S APPROACH TO SAFETY

I found more examples of high-stake industries with standards similar to the nuclear navy's. At an Orlando-area conference on safety, I met Greg Hale, VP and chief safety officer for Walt Disney Parks and Resorts. A brilliant man with over eighty US and foreign patents to his name, Hale began his current role more than twenty years ago. He told me about one of Disney's greatest failures that became the "never-again" impetus behind the company's now rigorous safety standards.

In 2003, unsecured bolts caused the locomotive of Disneyland's Big Thunder Mountain Railroad to derail and crash into the first passenger car, killing a twenty-two-year-old man. Hale, who was just a year into his role as chief safety officer, happened to be in California with his family when he heard the terrible news. He began his investigation into the cause immediately and determined then and there that Disney's safety standards must be transformed to ensure nothing like that could ever happen again. And in the two decades and hundreds of millions of rides Disney has given worldwide since then, no other fatal tragedy has occurred.

When I asked Hale about Disney's secrets of high reliability, what he shared sounded very familiar. First, Disney institutes exacting proactive safety standards with regular auditing to check for drift. Disney values transparency and shares safety lessons learned from park to park—not just from California to Florida, but across all Disney parks worldwide as well as amusement park competitors, like Six Flags. Safety committees continually run what-if scenarios, imagining what could go wrong and taking steps to ensure it doesn't. Disney's proactive safety measures include studying and learning from other industry accidents and near-misses, as well as implementing layers of auditing to find and reduce risk in their own operation.

I did not see evidence of these consistent safety standards in healthcare. But my team and I intended to change the narrative as Disney had done in 2003, to reject anything less than the highest of standards, and to eliminate preventable tragedies.

FIVE PILLARS OF HIGH RELIABILITY

We started by establishing five pillars of high reliability, based on Rickover's watch-standing principles. The first of these pillars, which are still used by the navy today, is a "higher level of understanding." It's important for clinicians to have technical expertise as well as critical thinking skills. This isn't possible without elevated understanding, continuous learning, and the sharing of lessons and knowledge.

The second pillar, "integrity," is both a personal and organizational standard. Each person must have the integrity to do the right thing in every situation, regardless of personal cost or recognition. The organization must show its integrity by providing employees the necessary tools. Clinicians must have the supplies, training, time, compensation, psychological support, and whatever else is needed to ensure they can perform their jobs at the highest possible levels.

The third pillar is "formality," meaning that rules must be respected, procedures followed, and workarounds eliminated. Teams must communicate and report information clearly. In the nuclear navy, for example, there are many standard procedures strictly followed without deviation and repeat backs used consistently to ensure all parties understand and agree with next steps.

The fourth pillar is a "questioning attitude." If something is unclear or doesn't look right, team members should ask about it (in other words, call the baby "ugly"). Research shows that when healthcare workers have concerns about the competence of a peer or supervisor, less than 3 percent will confront that person. If the potentially incompetent person is a physician, that number drops to less than 1 percent.[42] This reticence has to change. By risking a moment of awkwardness through questioning someone in authority and taking the chance of being wrong, a healthcare worker might literally save the life of a patient.

The fifth pillar is "backup." Having someone's back doesn't mean agreeing with everything that person says or does; it means doing what's needed to help that person succeed. Team members must be reliable as support, or sounding boards, and redirect other members when necessary. Remember my XO, Gary, on the *Texas*? He backed me up when I thought we were counter-detected. He rightly questioned my thinking, and I changed my planned order as a result. The fourth and fifth pillars rely on psychological safety, which in turn, relies on trust and love.

These pillars should be the bedrock of healthcare's daily operations. When they are, then everyone in the organization becomes a safety person. In the nuclear navy, the principles of high reliability are so ingrained that all but a few outliers have a safety mindset.

THREE MAJOR TOOLS

In addition to the pillars, our safety toolbox contained three major tools. The first was Speak Up for Safety (SUFS), a program that encouraged individuals to report safety issues and then recognized and celebrated those individuals for their initiative. This encouragement and recognition fostered a questioning attitude among workers and promoted psychological safety.

The second tool was Apparent Cause Analysis (ACA). This was a quick way to assess safety events by using the five pillars as a guide. ACA allowed us to identify root causes in a fraction of the time of a more traditional Root Cause Analysis (RCA) investigation, which typically took weeks. With the ACA, we could easily determine the root cause and implement short- and long-term corrective actions.

Third, we developed a method to share our findings. Team members used and reported SUFSs and ACAs almost daily, while safety officers at each campus collected the data and results. Once a month, my team would meet in person, discuss their most significant SUFS and ACA reports, and vote on the most pressing submissions. The team member whose submission was chosen would provide a brief presentation to a Quality, Safety, and Risk monthly collaboration meeting. The presentation would include recommendations for corrective action. Others in the meeting would share their thoughts and experiences. At the end of the meeting, we defined action items and identified the person or department most appropriate for addressing the issue. Since my team members were embedded in different campuses, they returned to their respective C-suite leaders to share lessons learned.

TOOLS IN ACTION

When patient safety officer Sharon Edwards learned a patient was given the wrong dosage of medication in the emergency department (ED), she began her investigation. Using the ACA form, Sharon noticed several places where our pillars of high reliability weren't followed.

Beds in the ED have scales that measure a patient's weight. Though the universal method of determining dosage is through the metric system, the bed scale in this instance was set to pounds.

The nurse who gave the dosage lacked understanding; she did not know she should use kilograms as the unit of measurement. She failed in formality by not following the standard operating procedure to measure the patient's weight correctly. She also didn't demonstrate integrity when she failed to look up the procedure she was unfamiliar with (or, perhaps, the organization lacked integrity by not ensuring the nurse had the proper training). When the weight seemed off, the nurse didn't exhibit a questioning attitude. Lastly, neither engineering nor the nurse's peers provided backup by double-checking the setting of the bed.

After Sharon identified the root cause of the mistake, she began to take corrective action by notifying the ED's engineering department and disseminating information to the clinical teams and C-suite leaders. Sharon also presented the ACA at our group's monthly collaborative meeting. There, we decided the issue should be shared at corporate's monthly performance and safety meeting with its 245 members from across the system. In this way, every clinical team on every campus was alerted to this potential safety issue.

Seems simple, but before ACAs, awareness of the problem would have been isolated to the ED it occurred in. Engineering would not even have been informed. The bed issue may not have been addressed at all if the ED team members were especially busy. In other words, the same issue could have easily occurred again with another patient receiving the wrong dosage, perhaps with deadly consequences.

Our new structure allowed us to broadcast the potential danger across fifty hospitals. However, that alone wasn't enough. We needed to take long-term corrective action. We went to the engineering team to identify the path that led to this failure. We examined the procurement and intake processes of hospital beds, and implemented a procedure to make sure the beds went through the proper checks. Then, we established a sustainment plan with conversation-based rounds to revisit the issue and ensure there was no drift from the appropriate weighing procedure. Finally, we tracked data on medication errors due to incorrect weights to monitor the implementation and success of the process. This is one of many examples of how the ACA and the sharing of best practices was successfully implemented when potentially dangerous problems arose.

UGLY BABIES

The newfound pattern of transparency was encouraging. Campuses learned from each other, procedures became standardized, and reporting continued to increase!

In addition, Speak Up for Safety and the ACAs were helping us to call the baby "ugly."

Every organization has ugly babies, and there's no shame in having them—only in failing to call them out. There's truth to the saying "It's not what you know, but when you knew it." If employees knew about a risk and didn't do something to prevent a future incident, they'd be at least partially responsible for the negative outcome.

Encouraging transparency and the pointing out of issues not only solves potential problems but also saves team members from culpability. This kind of focus on openness is actually a form of backup for one's team—a loving, protective act.

My team appreciated it when we received word of a possible problem before an incident occurred, but more often than not, concerns continued to be brought from risk management, after the fact.

One case involved actual babies and a very ugly problem. The birth care center of one of the campuses experienced three prenatal deaths in the course of a year, a concerning figure that likely had a contributing common cause. My team was dispatched to find it. Records, conversation rounds, and other investigative tools helped us to pinpoint one particular problem that indicated a departmental failure of integrity: a supply-chain issue. The elastic bands used to hold fetal monitors in place had gone up a bit in price, so the purchasing manager wasn't procuring the quantity needed. In some cases, patients were buying their own bands from online sources. In others, nurses were cutting up much more expensive back braces that were on hand and MacGyvering them to secure the fetal monitors. The lack of supplies made the medical staff feel overwhelmed and unsupported. The time nurses spent circumventing the problem pulled their attention away from more vital concerns.

Once we pinpointed and addressed the supply issue and instituted conversation-based rounds, the frenzy of the department began to dissipate. Even so, trust was not built back overnight. Like my initial attempts with the Crew Top Three on the *Texas*, reforming culture takes time and consistent follow-through. The sooner it begins, the better.

WORKPLACE SOCIAL MEDIA

While I continued in my role with the healthcare system, I began my pursuit of a doctorate from the Crummer Graduate School of Business at Rollins College. I decided to write my dissertation about an innovative communication device I was intrigued by. My healthcare organization had recently adopted a workplace social media tool (WSMT) to help develop culture, facilitate communication within the hospital system, and prevent staff burnout. The tool could be accessed through a network of touchscreen boards or through a smart phone, and it allowed leaders and frontline workers to communicate with each other in a transparent fashion. Problems like supply issues and equipment failures could be shared, as well as real-time solutions to various concerns. The system also gave leaders a platform to recognize their staff.

I loved the premise of the touchscreen boards, but I wanted to find out how they actually affected the quality of the staff's day-to-day work life. I hypothesized that the boards would improve relationships between leaders and staff, increase organizational trust and perceived organizational support (feeling valued by the organization), lower emotional exhaustion or burnout, and lower turnover intentions. ("Turnover intentions" speak to the likelihood of an employee leaving an organization in the near future. They are a more accurate measure of job satisfaction than actual turnover, which can occur for a multitude of reasons unrelated to job satisfaction, such as health and family concerns.)

I gleaned my data from 450 volunteers across four hospital campuses, who answered nearly fifty validated survey questions on the WSMT. My research confirmed my hypothesis. The boards did improve perceived organizational support, trust in the organization, and relationships. These improvements helped to reduce emotional exhaustion and turnover intentions.

No matter the size of a workplace, employees want to know that they matter. They want to be seen and heard. It's one thing to gather feedback from a submarine crew of 130 or so, but it's another challenge entirely to do this in an organization of over eighty thousand employees. But the WSMT shows that there are effective ways for even behemoth corporations to listen to the concerns of their employees, act on issues instead of ignoring them, and offer deserving employees system-wide recognition. In other words, organizations of any size can and should find creative ways to listen to and love their employees.

AN AUTHENTIC APOLOGY

Later, I gained a responsibility that resonated with my personal purpose. I began to teach struggling physicians how to develop healthy cultures with positive leadership.

One of my most memorable opportunities involved a verbally abusive surgeon. The Medical Staff (Med Staff), a board of physician leaders responsible for clinical oversight and patient safety, had reprimanded him many times. Inevitably, the more they intervened, the more defensive he became. The hospital was reluctant to let him go because he was an exemplary surgeon with incredibly high standards. Plus, turnover for surgeons costs millions. The Med Staff president called me as a last-ditch effort.

I listened to the staff on the receiving end of the unprofessional behavior, but I also listened to the surgeon—really listened. I asked about his frustrations, barriers, and personal issues. I wanted him to know I cared about him personally and professionally.

Once my picture of the situation was complete, I shared his concerns with his team and helped him find resolutions. I also shared the staff's apprehensions with the surgeon and brainstormed ways for him to build back their trust.

The surgeon had so severely broken the trust of his team that he needed to give an authentic apology before he could even start making reparations.

Issuing a true apology takes courage and vulnerability. The surgeon already felt raw from the continued interventions of the Med Staff, and he knew his head was on the proverbial chopping block. However, I'd shared stories about apologies I'd given in my own career and what a difference they had made to my team members. The surgeon trusted my advice and bravely addressed the group. He took responsibility for his actions and authentically showed regret.

The team's reaction was profound. Pain and relief came to the surface. One man left the room crying.

Obviously, the process couldn't end there. The surgeon couldn't apologize and then go back to his old ways. I wanted to help him address the issues that triggered his behavior, so members of my team began attending his surgical meetings. Our job was to make sure the surgical team members provided the tools the surgeon needed and the staff members were fully trained, so the surgeon could focus on his patients.

The first meetings were tense, and the team was skeptical. We began by stating expectations and finding solutions for roadblocks. As the group successfully addressed issues, the surgeon's demeanor grew increasingly relaxed, and eventually, the meetings became productive and filled with laughter.

It's been three years since the surgeon's apology, and he has continued to operate without any further complaints against him. This turnaround offers yet another testament to the power of building a healthy culture.

PET PEEVES

Often, investigating one problem uncovers another. The pounds-versus-kilograms issue appeared in the positron emission tomography (PET) lab as well, leading to inaccurate standard uptake values (SUVs) and the possibility of missing cancer in a patient scan.

Fortunately, the patients whose values had been entered incorrectly were cancer-free. However, the hospital had dodged a bullet, and the issue needed to be addressed.

I visited the PET lab to see what was causing the errors. The dark, cramped room was reminiscent of a submarine. The technician I shadowed spoke with kindness to her pediatric patient in the PET machine.

"Okay, love," she said, "please be still. If you move, this test will take longer."

Then the phone rang. "Good morning, PET lab. How can I help you?"

Looking back at the patient, "Please, love, stay still."

Back to the phone, "Yes, that's our location."

Back and forth it went. When the tech was finally finished with her patient and the phone calls and had a moment to speak with me, I fell back on my Crew Top Three technique, asking, "What bothers you when you come to work? What is your top concern?"

Her face grew taut, and her brow furrowed. Discarding the sweet tone she'd used for the child, the tech pointed her finger at me and said, "I'll tell you what bothers me! Leaders stop by all the time and ask how they can help me, and I tell them over and over again, but they do nothing about it!" She had no trust in the organization and no evidence of support.

My team and I investigated further and found numerous issues. In addition to technicians having to answer phones, patient procedures were being scheduled for insufficient periods of time, equipment was outdated, and there was poor coordination among departments. With the chaos in the lab, it was no wonder errors were being made.

We helped resolve the original kilogram issue and then moved on to fixing other problems, such as rerouting phones to the front desk and extending appointment times. Simple fixes like these went a long way toward regaining trust. Culture in the PET department improved as employees began to find their problems addressed, leading them to feel supported and cared for. It is no coincidence that error rates dropped significantly for at least four consecutive years following our intervention.

In the nuclear navy, we liked to celebrate events like the ones in the PET lab. We came together, shared lessons learned, and cheered for the fact that we'd caught a small-order deficiency before anyone was harmed. That was the attitude I strove to bring to healthcare and the focus I feel all industries should have. The goal is to solve problems, not assign guilt. It's to make team members feel valued, to do the right thing, and to lead with love. With this strategy, there will always be plenty of wins to celebrate.

— CHAPTER 20 —

Building Relationships

"Do what you can to show you care about other people, and you will make our world a better place."

—Rosalynn Carter

During my doctoral work, one of my professors, Dr. Greg Marshall, gave each student a theory to research. I was assigned the Leader-Member Exchange (LMX). When I dove into the theory, it was as if the heavens opened up and angels began to sing. It was exactly what I had believed and practiced all along, and now I had a name for it!

LEADER-MEMBER EXCHANGE

Developed by Dr. George B. Graen, LMX explains how leaders cultivate different types of exchanges, or relationships, with their team members. These exchanges can greatly affect the performance and engagement of both the members *and* the leaders. Repeated interactions between the two individuals strengthen a bond and form a symbiotic relationship in which each helps to solve problems for the other.[43]

This leadership theory is different from other theories such as servant leadership or transformational leadership, which focus more on the behavior of the leader. LMX measures the quality of the relationship between the leader and the member. It is the relationship that matters most in predicting outcomes. A mediocre workforce with high-quality relationships between leaders and team members can trump a more talented workforce lacking a strong LMX.

> A questionnaire called the LMX 7 was designed to quantify the strength of a relationship between a subordinate and leader. Respondents answer a series of seven questions on a scale of one to five. To me, the following question is the most revealing of the seven: "Regardless of the amount of formal authority your leader (follower) has, what are the chances that he or she would 'bail you out' at his or her expense?" This confidence (or lack of it) speaks volumes about the strength of the LMX relationship.[44]

LMX AT WORK

Looking back over my career, I can identify many examples of a high-quality LMX at work. The first that comes to mind was my relationship with Senior Chief Petty Officer Jeff Hiscocks on the *Texas*. Hiscocks was in charge of the auxiliary division, and he was one of the hardest-working and most talented sailors I have ever interacted with. His dedication and attitude made him an integral part of the submarine family, and he undoubtedly had my and the crew's back at the cost of his own, as did I for him.

During a scheduled thirty-five-day in-port maintenance period, we had planned preventative work on the main external hatches, which required complete disassembly, greasing, and reassembly. The Pearl Harbor Naval Shipyard had never conducted this type of maintenance on the hatches with their complex designs specific to our class of submarine.

As commanding officer, I didn't consider the task that difficult. But Hiscocks expressed serious concern over the complexity and potential pitfalls of the maintenance. Although we were the second Virginia-Class submarine, we were the first to attempt the process in Pearl Harbor. The senior chief understood that it wouldn't be a simple disassembly and reassembly linkage procedure. It would require hundreds of sequential steps with multiple pieces plus a rigorous sub-safe retest standard.

He asked to defer the maintenance to a more extended in-port maintenance period. But the shipyard and maintenance experts declined and gave us false promises that the maintenance would finish on time.

Even though I respected Hiscocks's opinion, I deferred to the shipyard. But the shipyard was wrong, and so was I. The evolution took longer, as Senior Chief Hiscocks had predicted, delaying our underway period by two weeks. Due to the delay, our major engineering inspection, the Operational Reactor Safeguards Exam, had to be rescheduled.

The new inspection time period with workup conflicted with Hiscocks's previously approved vacation. It was time he intended to spend with his relatives, who had already purchased an expensive trip to Hawaii.

We considered Hiscocks an integral part of the success of our engineering exam, and he understood the difficulty of this short period at sea without him. So when I broke the news to the crew, I could see his disappointment. He assumed he had no choice but to miss this once-in-a-lifetime event with his family.

I called Hiscocks to my stateroom and told him, "You're staying behind. You need to be with your family."

He looked at me in disbelief.

"No, I can't," he said.

"Yes, you can, but do me a favor and make sure your team is well trained. Get your records squared away. I could not appreciate you more. If it weren't for you, we would not have the great team we have today. You make such a difference to so many."

As we pulled away for the ten-day underway, I saw Hiscocks standing on the pier. He spotted me where I stood on top of the sail of the submarine and our eyes connected. He had a huge smile on his face and an expression of gratitude. Our interaction had not only strengthened our own LMX, leading to a positive outcome for both of us, it also strengthened my LMX with other members of the crew who had witnessed it.

LMX is much more than a simple transaction. It's about agape love and family-like relationships in which people will risk themselves for others. Hiscocks always did his best for me by going above and beyond in all his work. In return, I did my best for him by honoring his vacation time, even if it meant we'd do worse on the engineering exam. Was it the right decision? Absolutely! Without a doubt. Hiscocks again upheld his part of the relationship by ensuring his department was well prepared. We scored the highest possible grade in his division. And since future leaders had the opportunity to fill in for Hiscocks and gain valuable experience, it ended up being a win-win situation.

The LMX I shared with Hiscocks contrasted sharply with another relationship I had during that same period. I remember attending a *sayonara* party for a visiting Japanese submarine, which I would have missed without that same preventative maintenance delay. The SUBPAC, a two-star admiral in the Pacific Fleet and over that shipyard, made a sarcastic comment to me about the *Texas* still being in port. Despite his little chuckle, I knew he didn't mean it as a joke. The comment hurt. Though his shipyard didn't deliver on its scheduling promise, the fault lay with me as CO. His derision made me feel like an object rather than a person. Needless to say, the quality of our LMX remained low.

FAMILY AND FLYING FISH

In early 2021, a worldwide trend began in which masses of people voluntarily resigned from their jobs. The phenomenon, dubbed "the Great Resignation" by Professor Anthony Klotz, is ongoing and a clear indication to me that employees feel less needed.[45] The average person *wants* a sense of belonging. The more a person feels connected, the more they care. And when someone becomes emotionally invested in a team and a company, they'll give the best they have to give.

There are those who don't think work associates and family can be compared. Organizational psychologist David Burkus writes, "Calling your company a family may be a well-meaning metaphor, but it's not useful. Most employees don't want to be part of another family."[46] I couldn't disagree more—and I'm not alone.

In his 2004 book, *When Fish Fly*, John Yokoyama recounts his change of thinking as a leader and the transformation that came from it. Yokoyama bought a small, open-air fish market in the 1960s, where he and his staff worked long, hard hours. Over the years, his business did well, but his employees complained and gossiped. What's more, they didn't trust him. Yokohama reflected on the problem and spent time in self-examination. He realized that he had been treating his employees like they were replaceable objects rather than people, let alone family.

He determined to improve the situation and began seeking his employees' feedback through a process similar to the Crew Top Three. Though not all of his team's ideas made the cut, many did, including the suggestion to reduce work hours, which didn't even hurt profitability. Yokohama also tackled the gossip and complaints about others' work habits by encouraging veteran employees to coach newer teammates. The culture shift at the fish market was palpable.

Today, Pike Place Market in Seattle is not only world-famous for the fishmonger who throws fish, but also for the way Yokohama established trust and transparency with his work family.[47]

TSP MODEL

The day I left the *Texas*, I felt a strong sense of accomplishment—not for the missions achieved or awards won, but for the family we had built and the love we shared. We'd made a habitual and deliberate practice of caring for each other, and we'd demonstrated this through our trust, standards, and purpose (TSP). I believe this trifecta is evidence of love in action in the workplace. Love alone wouldn't have gotten my crew through our Arctic operation. We had to establish TSP.

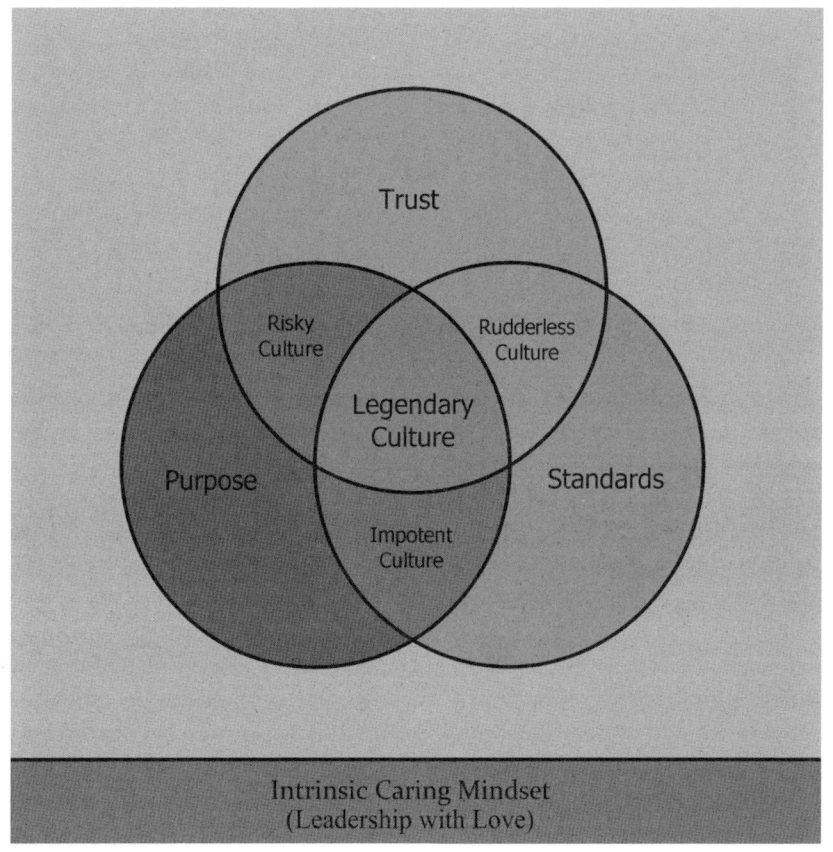

TSP Model

TSP is the lifeblood of a game-changing culture. It's essential to examine these elements closely to truly comprehend how they work in perfect synchronization. Where all three circles of the above Venn diagram come together, magic happens. But if even one element of TSP is missing, the outcome will fall flat.

TRUST

When standards and purpose combine without trust, the culture becomes impotent. A team member who is neither trusted nor given any reason to trust their leader will not go above and beyond their normal duties. They might even leave tasks incomplete or hide problems. Think of the Seawolf-class submarine that I rode as a PCOI. Because the CO didn't care about his men, they didn't feel compelled to fix the air compressors. On the *West Virginia*, no one wanted to tell MFB that the ship was heading in the wrong direction because they didn't trust that his reaction would be fair. In both cases, the crew understood the standards and their mission, but without trust, no one cared about the standards, or even the ultimate success of their mission.

Trust is "the extent to which one is willing to ascribe good intentions to and have confidence in the words and actions of other people."[48] With trust, people are willing to do more to extend themselves, because while they operate under that trust, there's no high cost of failure. But trust takes time to develop, requiring affirmative words and active follow-through demonstrated with reliability and consistency.

STANDARDS

When trust and purpose combine without standards, the culture becomes risky. A leader can be trusted, and a team might understand their purpose, but if they don't have standards to guide how things should be done, unsafe conditions occur. Remember the *Indianapolis*? The crew had a mission, to deliver top-secret cargo essential to the war effort. *And* the crew trusted their captain. But the standards of the day were not upheld. Whether zig-zagging would have actually protected the ship against the enemy torpedo or not is unclear, but the lack of standards had devastating consequences for the CO's reputation, career, and, ultimately, his mental well-being.

In order to uphold standards as a CO, I consistently shared my command philosophy, making sure every sailor understood it. I even instituted rules that were more rigorous than the navy required—for example, my 20 percent drug-testing policy—but that higher bar was for the good of the ship and for the shipmates themselves.

I also didn't impose standards for the sake of standards. Rather, I implemented caring expectations fueled by love.

PURPOSE

Lastly, when trust and standards combine without purpose, the culture becomes rudderless. A team will not have guideposts or a goal to offer direction. Consider a submarine's culinary specialist. They may understand the high standards demanded of them and even trust their sub's command, but without knowing how vital good food is to keeping the crew healthy and happy, the cook may decide they aren't really that important. They might even neglect certain aspects of their job. After all, it would be easy to feel insignificant while peeling potatoes or mopping floors. Purpose can give even menial tasks importance and value.

One of the patient safety nurses I worked with in the healthcare system was clear on her purpose. She shared a quote with me and said, "This is my 'why.'" The quote was by Dr. Donald M. Berwick, cofounder of the Institute for Healthcare Improvement:

> [The names of the patients whose lives we save] can never be known. Our contribution will be what did not happen to them. And, though they are unknown, we will know that mothers and fathers are at graduations and weddings they would have missed, and that grandchildren will know grandparents they might never have known, and holidays will be taken, and work completed, and books read, and symphonies heard, and gardens tended that, without our work, would have been only beds of weeds.[49]

"Every time I hear or read this quote," the nurse said, "it brings tears to my eyes. I reflect on all of the patients I've seen pass over the years, parents I've comforted after the passing of their children, and patients I've seen overcome illness. These experiences push me harder and harder every day to accomplish our mission and do no harm."

Her understanding of purpose and belief in her ability to change lives rates a ten out of ten. I loved her passion for her work, and I wish that same passion for everyone.

APOLOGY AND EMPATHY

A leader who has a caring mindset, has set standards, and has clearly defined purpose is well on their way to creating a legendary culture. But humility is important too. A leader needs to acknowledge the possibility that they may be part of the problem. When a concern is brought to my attention, I must look in the mirror and see what part I played in the situation. What standard, training, or cultural issue did I cause that contributed to the problem? Then, I must apologize, like I did on the *Texas*, for example, when I found out my crew didn't have enough computers.

A good leader shows empathy. It's critically important to remember that employees are people, not commodities. Many of the "what not to do" examples from my past—and even some I encounter now—stemmed from leaders who lacked empathy. I often think of the sailor with the lanyard on the USS *Asheville*. If Captain Fenwick had taken just a moment to consider the time and expense that young man had put into making the lanyard and the pride he had in the result, Fenwick might have rethought his flippant comment about the colors the sailor had chosen.

LOVE RECIPROCATED

Loving leadership will reward you in ways you never expect. What you receive in return will feel exponentially more than what you give.

In preparing for this book, my editor reached out to some who had served under me for their perspectives. Jared Mankins, the officer who'd needed an adjusted schedule to keep his appointment at the fertility clinic, described my leadership style this way:

> Captain was always involved, asking about our lives, our families, goals, careers, etc., the way a father would be. He knew our wives' and kids' names, even some of our birthdays . . . all of it. You could tell him about something going on in your life, get pulled away from that conversation, and a couple of weeks later, he would pick it back up like nothing had happened. He remembered right where you left off.
>
> There were things that you'd tell your chief about your personal life, and Bob would ask you about them later, just to make sure you were being taken care of. I can honestly say that he cared, it wasn't just a face or a way of leading, you could tell it was him as a person that truly cared about the crew. That mentality carried down into the XO, the engineer, and the rest of the wardroom as well. It really made it feel like a family and made me dread disappointing him or anyone else in the chain. That fear of disappointment wasn't a fear of getting in trouble or mast or discipline. It was a fear similar to what I feel with my dad, the desire to make him proud and not wanting to disappoint him in that regard.

He cared more about the people than the job, and that made the people want to do everything they could not to disappoint him. He demanded excellence, but not in that angry fist-pounding kind of way you see in movies. He wanted people to be their best with no excuses. His no-victim mentality pushed people not to make or accept excuses, but to just find or make a way to get done what needed to get done.

Jared's words touched me to my core. As a leader, I always hoped to leave a legacy of love. I never expected to reap such rich dividends, though. Helping Jared and his wife in a small way to start their family is one of the most cherished moments of my career. Tears filled my eyes the first time I saw a picture of their daughter.

I couldn't help thinking how good things lead to a good life. We often focus on the big stuff—complicated projects, dangerous missions, lofty positions—and don't think much of the daily interruptions thrown our way. But if we make a habit of doing the right thing, of building relationships and doing the best we can for others, we are guaranteed to get back the most life has to offer.

―CHAPTER 21―

Final Thoughts

"Rules are for the obedience of fools and the guidance of wise men."

—Harry Day

As I neared the tail end of writing this book, I happened to read *Good to Great* by Jim Collins. Collins and his team "systematically scoured a list of 1,435 established companies to find every extraordinary case that made a leap from no-better-than-average results to great results."[50] Despite having virtually identical opportunities with comparable organizations, eleven companies averaged returns nearly seven times higher than the market.[51]

LEVEL 5 LEADERS

Over the course of five years, Collins and his team discovered that each of these companies was led by what they termed a "Level 5 leader." Level 5 leaders possess four common leadership characteristics—being a highly capable individual, a contributing team member, a competent manager, and an effective leader—plus a little something extra. That "something extra" is born from a combination of personal humility and professional will.

Level 5 leaders are modest. If there's fault to be had, they accept it, but they're quick to pass praise onto others. Collins and his team call this "the window and the mirror" and describe it this way:

If [Level 5 leaders] can't find a specific person or event to give credit to, they credit good luck. At the same time, they look in the mirror to assign responsibility, never citing bad luck or external factors when things go poorly.[52]

Inferior leaders do just the opposite. The irony is that the mirror and the window perspective doesn't reflect reality. "Level 5 leaders *were* responsible for their companies' transformations. But they would never admit that."[53]

Collins describes four disciplines that Level 5 leaders practice. First, they attend to their people before their strategy: "Get the right people on the bus and the wrong people off."[54] (Sounds very similar to my rowers in a boat analogy, doesn't it?)

Next, they confront the tough facts of their reality while maintaining faith that they will prevail. (They value transparency and call the baby "ugly" when necessary.)

Level 5 leaders also make breakthroughs by maintaining consistent effort. (Winning the trust of the *Texas* crew and thereby changing the culture happened only by showing them time and time again that their feedback would receive a positive response.)

Finally, these top-tier leaders understand what Collins terms "the Hedgehog Concept" and position their companies at the sweet spot where the answers to these three considerations intersect: What are we deeply passionate about? What can we be the best in the world at? What drives our economic engine?[55] Notice how the three categories of the TSP model line up? The first question of the Hedgehog Concept relates to purpose; the second, to standards (the foundation of excellence); and the third, to trust. Particularly within high-stakes industries, trust is essential to safety and mission success. Thus, it drives the economic engine.

So much of what I've learned has come from the examples of the type of Level 5 leader Collins describes. With personal humility and professional will, Hyman G. Rickover and Bruce Grooms led their teams to greatness.

Though *Good to Great* has sold millions of copies in the twenty-two years since it was published, detractors of Collins's theories point out that the eleven companies Collins highlighted haven't continued to remain "great" but rather, as a whole, have underperformed the S&P 500.[56] However, Collins doesn't think the companies' downturn in performance negates his team's findings. Instead, he believes the negative change stems from a shift in culture and attitude. In his book *How the Mighty Fall*, Collins states, "Just because a company falls doesn't invalidate what we can learn by studying that company when it was at its historical best."[57]

Though I don't believe there's any recipe for success with a no-fail guarantee, the findings that grew out of the *Good to Great* team's five years of study so closely mirror my own observations and experience that I can't help but think them valid and instructive.

LIFE IS FOR SERVICE

I've shared many stories about the leaders I've served under, as well as the skills I've gathered and adapted for my own leadership toolbox. But the task of learning is never done. As I have continued to develop, I have found other examples of leadership and love that have resonated with me, including the most famous graduate of my alma mater, Rollins College.

He was a humble man from Pittsburgh, who spent his career teaching children about feelings, friendship, and life. As a student, Fred Rogers was inspired by a motto engraved in marble near Rollins's Strong Hall: "Life Is for Service." He carried a photo of the plaque in his wallet for the rest of his days to remind him of his purpose.[58]

Rediscovering the wisdom of Mister Rogers at my age has been eye-opening, and I am not alone in this rediscovery. In the twenty years since his death, all things Mister Rogers have made a resurgence—not among children, but adults. Why have the soft-spoken words of a children's television show host come to matter to so many? Jeff Monroe writes about the phenomenon: "He's calm. He's patient. He's kind. He's loving ... We are so hungry for love, we simply cannot get enough of it when we see it. We are starved for grace to know we are accepted just as we are and sit transfixed when we hear Mister Rogers tell us he wants to be [our] neighbor."[59]

One of Mister Roger's famous quotes aligns with the heart of my own mission: "Love and success, always in that order. It's that simple AND that difficult."[60]

THE GOOD LIFE

I've also gained inspiration and valuable wisdom from things I've read. Years ago, as I was preparing for a long deployment and looking for an interesting book to take with me, I came across Charles Colson's *The Good Life*. Of course, it piqued my curiosity; being away from my own family so often made me question if I was actually living a good life.

The premise of Colson's book was simple: to lead a good life, you need to help others. The car that you drive won't give you a good life. Neither will fame, your work title, or education. The beautiful thing about achieving a good life is that it's so simple—we all have the ability to do it.

Colson writes about the final scenes of the World War II movie *Saving Private Ryan*. Captain John H. Miller, played by Tom Hanks, leads a unit charged with locating Private James Ryan and returning him home safely. All of Ryan's brothers had just perished in the war, and military leadership decided Ryan's family needed their last remaining son returned home. After finding Ryan, a harrowing gun battle ensues, leaving Miller, along with many of his men, dead or fatally wounded. With his last breath, the captain tells Ryan, "James . . . Earn this. Earn it!"[61]

Later, a much older Ryan reflects on the enormity of the sacrifices Captain Miller's unit made to find him. He is filled with emotion as he stands at the Normandy American Cemetery with his family looking on. Addressing Miller's headstone, Ryan says, "Every day, I think about what you said to me that day on the bridge, and I've tried to live my life the best I could. I hope that was enough. I hope that, at least in your eyes, I earned what all of you have done for me."

Then Ryan pleads with his wife, "Tell me I've led a good life."

Perplexed, she says, "What?"

"Tell me I am a good man," he says.

"You are," she answers.

The scene spoke to me. It reminded me of why I care so much for those under my charge. It reminded me of my father. I thought of all the things he went without in his early years and of how hard he worked to give us the things he never had. He found fulfillment in providing for his family and watching us benefit from his hard work. He was the first person who taught me the joy of caring for the well-being of others and leading with love.

THE ULTIMATE SERVANT LEADER

My final and best example is Jesus. Although I'm not a particularly religious man, I truly believe Jesus was the ultimate servant leader. He cared about the concerns of those around him, healing mothers-in-law and helping wedding hosts save face. And he didn't seek praise or glory, opting for a donkey ride over a kingly entrance into Jerusalem when his popularity was at its height. Just a few days after his humble procession, he kicked off the last meal he'd share with his apostles by kneeling before them and washing their twelve pairs of stinky feet:

> You call me "Teacher" and "Lord," and rightly so, for that is what I am. Now that I, your Lord and Teacher, have washed your feet, you

also should wash one another's feet. I have set you an example that you should do as I have done for you.[62]

Despite all the other things that were on the cusp of happening—the betrayal of a friend, abandonment from his followers, and ultimately, death—Jesus used the last moments of quality time he had with his crew to emphasize the importance of service to others. I believe it was his most significant lesson for them and for us still today.

A NEW DIRECTION

Before wrapping up this chapter and book with my distilled list of leadership advice, I must return to the memoir side of things.

In 2019, the Florida Chamber of Commerce decided to work toward the goal of making Florida the safest state in the country. The chamber formed a safety council with representatives from various companies in the area, such as Coca Cola, Florida Blue, ABC Fine Wine & Spirits, Nautique Boats, and Disney, to name a few. I was chosen as the representative of the healthcare system to sit on the safety council.

Soon, the chamber began to dream bigger. Florida is currently the sixteenth largest economy in the world, recently surpassing Saudi Arabia, and about to overtake Indonesia. The chamber adopted the goal to make Florida's economy the tenth largest by 2030.[63]

Achieving a flourishing economy requires a flourishing workforce. To address the needs of Florida's workforce, the chamber established a leadership cabinet with three areas of focus: safety, health, and sustainability. I was given charge of the health pillar. However, it quickly became evident that they needed someone who could offer more than a mere five or so volunteer hours per week to really move the needle. There was just so much to be done!

When chamber leadership began discussing the possibility of creating the full-time position of senior vice president to head the Florida Chamber Health Council, with a special focus on a statewide, business-led, mental healthcare initiative, I considered filling the role myself.

The struggles faced by both of my parents have made improving mental healthcare a passion project for me. The position would offer me influence throughout the state and the ability to help more people lead a good life. I expressed my interest and was chosen for the role, which I began on May 1, 2023.

In many ways, I am starting from scratch with this latest (and hopefully last) career pivot. But the importance of this work resonates with me like nothing else ever has. I believe it is my calling and purpose in life, and I am incredibly thankful for the journey that led me to this spot and for the learning I experienced along the way.

And now, as promised, that list of lessons . . .

WHAT WOULD NAVY BOB DO?

My former deputy, Mike Majewski, later became the Squadron Seven Commodore, just as I had been. While serving in the role, he told me he had a sticky note attached to his computer that said "WWNBD?"—which stood for "What would Navy Bob do?" I use Majewski's question here (with tongue firmly in cheek) as I offer a summation of my thoughts on leadership:

Define your purpose. Remind your people often where you are headed together and how their individual contributions help the team to fulfill its purpose.

Develop trust. Start by gathering feedback about your team's concerns. (I recommend the Crew Top Three.) Address concerns promptly and publicly, then do your best to rectify them. Be transparent—even when issues can't be easily resolved.

Create and communicate caring standards, explain the reasoning behind those standards, and enforce them consistently.

Understand that training breeds confidence and personal excellence leads to success.

Seek trusted sources to reveal your blind spots. Accept your responsibility for failures and apologize authentically.

Treat your team like family. Demonstrate empathy, compassion, and respect.

Always be willing to jump in and offer aid.

Live and breathe the five pillars of high reliability: a higher level of understanding, integrity, formality, a questioning attitude, and backup.

Demonstrate humility. Be quick to accept blame, but pass praise onto others.

Emulate great leaders. Reflect on what caused poor leaders to fail.

Be driven toward good with the "courageous impatience" of Rickover.

Ask yourself, "What's the right thing to do?"

Above all, love.

Epilogue

Over the years, I have gathered untold lessons from many great leaders. The one that means the most to me is the importance of sacrificial love. With every fiber of my being, I believe this is the true secret to any type of success. It is by serving others that we are able to thrive as families, communities, organizations, and countries across the globe.

I truly hope that what I've learned will be shared, the foundational aspects of culture will be implemented, and magical environments will be multiplied beyond the sea. I have seen how a culture of love can transform lives and impact teams, large and small, and I hope you, my readers, will see that too.

I have been blessed to fill many roles that have enabled me to help others and make a positive impact. My work in healthcare allowed me to leverage what I learned about culture in the navy and extend it into a radically different arena.

In my new season of life with the Florida Chamber Health Council, I hope to help Florida become the safest, healthiest, and most sustainable state in the country. I've also begun teaching at University of Central Florida's College of Community Innovation and Education School of Global Health Management and Informatics, where I have the good fortune to shape future generations of leaders.

I can't say what I'll be doing years down the road, but wherever I am, I plan to continue to share my experiences and underscore the importance of trust, standards, and purpose for building cultures and improving outcomes.

As Mister Rogers said in his Marquette University commencement address, "It's a miracle when we finally discover whom we're best equipped to serve, when we can best appreciate the unique life we've been given."[64] I hope this book inspires you to use your gifts to help others and to lead your teams with love.

Acknowledgments

I'd like to begin by thanking my editors, Stacey Tol, Darren Sapp, and Tracey Mastrapa. Stacey, you are an inspiration and I'm so grateful for your expertise. Darren, thank you for helping me begin this journey and get my thoughts in order. Tracey, thank you for your work and for encouraging me to dig deeper.

To Stephanie, my wife of over thirty years, thank you for bringing it all together and for being my sounding board. I love you more than anything. You have always been there for me and continue to support my dreams and goals to help others.

Next, I'd like to thank my children, Sophia and Zack, for the sacrifices you made by allowing me to pursue a military career, for standing strong through moves and deployments, and for tolerating me as I went back to school. I missed out on quite a few birthdays, holidays, and sporting events, but you remained supportive and understanding. I can't express how proud I am of both of you!

I appreciate every leader I have ever had for all the good and not-so-good lessons they have taught me. It's no surprise that I owe the biggest debt to Admiral Bruce Grooms. Thank you, Admiral Grooms, for giving me my first real work family at a time I desperately needed it, and for your continued support and encouragement. I also want to offer a special thank you to President George W. Bush and Mrs. Laura Bush for your unselfish leadership and unwavering love for this great country and its citizens.

I served with so many amazing officers and enlisted, and they have all left lasting impressions on me. There are more than I can name, but I need to highlight a few. First, my extraordinary XO and friend, Gary Montalvo. Thanks, Gary, for having my back, sharing my vision, and helping to make *Texas* the best family on the waterfront. Thank you, Mike Majewski, for your continued encouragement, hard work, and commitment to the people. You understand the mission on the job and in life. Jared Mankins, thanks for your feedback for this book and allowing me to share your story. Thank you, Carlos Martinez, Scott Bresnahan, Ryan Shirley, Cameron Lindsey, Jeff Cornellie, Rory Wohlgumuth, Matt Harris, Courtney Roach, Richard Nickols, Matt Lasher, Joshua Phillips, Shane Hollander, and Jeff Hiscocks. To my entire *Texas* crew, you continue to make me proud.

I would also like to thank Bobby Irish and Mike Wilkerson for taking the time to provide me with their input. You are true shipmates. Also, I'd like to acknowledge Greg Roach, Tom Cain, Eddie Robledo, Bob Robinson, Scott Jackson, Craig Soleim, Tim Pew, and Steve Shiring for riding some of the storms with me!

I have had the pleasure to serve with many more outstanding leaders. A shout-out to Jeff Zeuner, Butch Dolloga, Rob Gaucher, Jeff Jablon, Brian Howes, Dennis Murphy, Mike McKinnon, Lee Hankins, Bob Brandhuber, Daniel Futch, Joe Campbell, Pete Hildreth, Andy Domina, and the late Glen Niederhauser. I am deeply grateful for the lifelong friendships we have developed, all because the navy brought us together.

To my former MILAIDES, Mark "Ziggy" Thompson, Daniel "Scrub" Walsh, Keith Davids, Curtis Buzzard, Tom McCarthy, Jeff Gagnier, Gina Humble, and Clay Beers, it was an honor to work with such top-notch talent. Your continued friendships mean the world to me. To the Secret Service and White House friends, including Mark Fox, Ray Spicer, George Mulligan, Dan Donahue, Joe Clancy, Mickey Nelson, Cindy Wright, John Meyers, Jason Recher, Jared Weinstein, Paul Morris, Eric Draper, Shealah Craighead, Robert Favela, and Ronny Jackson, thanks for your friendship and continuous support! I'd like to make a special callout to the Peloton One riders, whose friendships I cherish and appreciate.

My Maritime brothers, you have given me the best stories and friendships a person could ever ask for! Thank you, Eric Stolzenberg, Chuck Rockwell, James Sagar, Tim Klaybor, Chris Webb, Chris Hughes, Pat Roach, Drew Hodgens, Jim McEntaggert, the late Vic Sammons, and my other college mates. Our time together still brings a smile to my face and an occasional belly laugh. I can't leave out my Dunkirk High School class of 1987, who continue to support me to this day, including Sue Rusch, Dave Swift, TJ Gibbons, Alice Domst, Joe Gugino, Dara Sage, Mary Forbes, and Eddie Aniszewski. Also, to Coach Jim Gibbons and John Bogardus: you've influenced me in ways great and small.

My healthcare journey would not have been possible without the love and support of so many. Thank you, Dr. Jeffrey Kuhlman and Dr. Dave Moorhead, for starting me on the path, and Dr. Neil Finkler, for guiding me as I went. Thank you to my safety team—Karina Coapstick, Jaclyn Jeffries, Tania Aylmer, Sam Miller, Grace Lai, Sharon Edwards, Teresa Tomlinson, Kya Andrews, Lauryn Verica, Soryda Rodriguez, Nicole Sneed, and Angela Victor—who went into the healthcare battle with me. We made a difference in the lives of so many.

Thank you to Rollins College and the professors, including Dr. Greg Marshall, Dr. J. Fernando Jaramillo, and Dr. Henrique Correa, who opened my eyes to research and the Leader-Member Exchange. Thank you, Dr. George. B. Graen, not only for your amazing scholarly work and your LMX theory, but also for becoming my good friend. I cherish your counsel. To my friends and colleagues Dr. Elvis Carnero and Ron Fleisher, thank you for your help and support.

Thank you to the Florida Chamber of Commerce for the opportunity to serve in my new role.

Finally, my parents. The way they both cared for and nurtured me allowed me to grow into the person I am today. Though my father has passed away, he is still an inspiration to me, and I can never repay him for his love and sacrifice. Thank you, Mom and Dad.

Appendix

USS *TEXAS* COMMAND PHILOSOPHY

From: Commanding Officer, USS *Texas* (SSN 775)
To: All Hands
Subject: Command Philosophy

This memorandum describes my command philosophy and establishes my expectations of every *Texas* crew member. It is the people that separate one submarine from the next and my philosophy is centered on enabling our people to achieve their full potential.

TAKING CARE OF SHIPMATES. Taking care of you personally and professionally will be one of my highest priorities. I will routinely ask for your input to improve our efficiency and our overall quality of life onboard *Texas*.

HAVE PRIDE IN YOURSELF, HAVE PRIDE IN YOUR SHIP. Personal excellence is a cornerstone of every successful command. The standards you uphold, the cleanliness of your space, your personal appearance, your conduct and demeanor—these are all reflections of your personal pride.

KNOW YOUR SHIP, KNOW YOUR MISSION. BE COMPETENT AND CONFIDENT. We must all have the technical competence to operate and maintain the ship to keep it combat ready. From competence comes confidence, and you need these together to achieve excellence. Utilize every opportunity, especially at sea, to effectively train.

TREAT EACH OTHER WITH RESPECT AND DIGNITY. We are a team and everyone is a contributing member. We do not harass, haze, or ridicule each other or tolerate anyone who does. I consider the basic respect for authority and human dignity paramount to *Texas*'s good order and discipline. Don't say or do to a crewmember what you would not want said or done to you.

HAVE STRENGTH OF CHARACTER. Integrity, loyalty, and courage are the character attributes that I hold in highest esteem. Lead by example and do not compromise your character for short-term gain. This ship cannot function without men of strong moral foundation and character. We trust our lives to each other, and I expect every man to commit himself to upholding the highest standards in this area.

DO NOT BE A VICTIM. We can control our own destiny. You can make your own luck. When there are problems, do not look outside the ship to point a finger. Rather, look inside to those things we can control—and change—to improve our position.

We can never lose sight of the fact that we serve on the most complex warship in the world that spends most of its time operating hundreds of feet beneath the sea. We are highly trained to do this, but we must always strive to be better. We either get better or worse, we don't stay the same. I do not ask for perfection. However, I do demand that you give me your best effort in everything that you do, and I will do the same. Together we can make *Texas* the best submarine in the Fleet.

R. A. RONCSKA

Endnotes

1. Joep Metz, "Can Leadership Be Taught—A Study about Leadership Development in Education," (master's thesis, Linnaeus University, 2015), https://lnu.diva-portal.org/smash/record.jsf?pid=diva2%3A819317&dswid=-634.

2. 1 Cor. 13:4-8 (NIV)

3. Phil Jackson and Hugh Delehanty, *Sacred Hoops: Spiritual Lessons of a Hardwood Warrior (Revised)* (New York: Hachette Go, 2006), 21.

4. "Hyman G. Rickover," Atomic Heritage Foundation, accessed June 19, 2023, https://ahf.nuclearmuseum.org/ahf/profile/hyman-g-rickover/.

5. Theodore Rockwell, *The Rickover Effect: How One Man Made a Difference* (Lincoln, NE: iUniverse, 2002), 265.

6. David Hoffman, "Submarine: Steel Boats, Iron Men," September 9, 2018, YouTube video, 56:11, https://www.youtube.com/watch?v=7Qt7dyhB-jg.

7. Hyman G. Rickover, "Doing a Job," (speech, Columbia University School of Engineering, November 5, 1981), ValidLab, accessed July 27, 2023, https://www.validlab.com/administration/rickover.html.

8. James Conca, "How the U.S. Navy Remains the Masters of Modular Nuclear Reactors," *Forbes*, December 23, 2019, https://www.forbes.com/sites/jamesconca/2019/12/23/americas-nuclear-navy-still-the-masters-of-nuclear-power/?sh=3e1da5a46bcd.

9   Karl Albrecht, "The (Only) 5 Fears We All Share," BrainSnacks (blog), *Psychology Today*, March 22, 2012, https://www.psychologytoday.com/us/blog/brainsnacks/201203/the-only-5-fears-we-all-share.

10 Hyun Duck-Kim and Angelita Bautista Cruz, "Transformational Leadership and Psychological Well-Being of Service-Oriented Staff: Hybrid Data Synthesis Technique," *International Journal of Environmental Research and Public Health* 19, no. 13 (July 4, 2022): 8189, https://doi.org/10.3390/ijerph19138189.

11 Simon Sinek (@SimonSinek), "Leaders are not responsible for the results. Leaders are responsible for the people who are responsible for the results," Twitter, March 22, 2015, 8:52 a.m., https://twitter.com/simonsinek/status/712260688941617152?lang=en.

12 Simon Sinek, "Trust vs. Performance," November 17, 2022, YouTube video, 2:27, https://www.youtube.com/watch?v=PTo9e3ILmms.

13 Sinek, "Trust vs. Performance."

14 Daniel Coyle, *The Culture Code: The Secrets of Highly Successful Groups* (New York: Bantam Books, 2018), 140.

15 "Research Starters: Worldwide Deaths in World War II," The National World War II Museum New Orleans, accessed June 12, 2023, https://www.nationalww2museum.org/students-teachers/student-resources/research-starters/research-starters-worldwide-deaths-world-war; "Killed, Wounded, and Missing," Britannica, accessed June 12, 2023, https://www.britannica.com/event/World-War-I/Killed-wounded-and-missing.

16 "List of Wars by Death Toll," Wikipedia, accessed June 12, 2023, https://en.wikipedia.org/wiki/List_of_wars_by_death_toll#Charts_and_graphs.

17 George W. Bush, "Statement by the President in His Address to the Nation," news release, September 11, 2001, The White House Archives, accessed June 23, 2023, https://georgewbush-whitehouse.archives.gov/news/releases/2001/09/20010911-16.html.

18 George W. Bush, "Address Before a Joint Session of the Congress on the State of the Union," The American Presidency Project, January 31, 2006, https://www.presidency.ucsb.edu/documents/address-before-joint-session-the-congress-the-state-the-union-13.

19 Bush, "Address Before a Joint Session."

20 Karl Rove, *Courage and Consequence: My Life as a Conservative in the Fight* (New York: Threshold Editions, 2010), 108-109.

21 George H. W. Bush, "Inaugural Address of George Bush," The Avalon Project, Lillian Goldman Law Library of Yale Law School, January 20, 1989, https://avalon.law.yale.edu/20th_century/bush.asp.

22 Dean Keith Simonton, "Presidential IQ, Openness, Intellectual Brilliance, and Leadership: Estimates and Correlations for 42 U.S. Chief Executives," *Political*

Psychology 27, no. 4 (August 2006): 511-526, https://onlinelibrary.wiley.com/doi/10.1111/j.1467-9221.2006.00524.x.

23 "Lieutenant Michael P. Murphy (SEAL)," America's Navy, accessed June 12, 2023, https://www.navy.mil/MEDAL-OF-HONOR-RECIPIENT-MICHAEL-P-MURPHY/.

24 "Lieutenant Michael P. Murphy (SEAL)."

25 Douglas MacArthur, *Reminiscences* (New York: McGraw-Hill, 1964), 82.

26 "Captain Gary Montalvo," Submarine Force Pacific, COMSUBDEVRON FIVE, accessed June 23, 2023, https://www.csp.navy.mil/csds5/Leadership/commodore/.

27 Shaun Griffin, "USS North Carolina Holds Change of Command," DVIDS, January 20, 2017, https://www.dvidshub.net/news/220876/uss-north-carolina-holds-change-command.

28 Gary Montalvo, "Submarine Commanding Officer Reflects on Leadership Lessons Learned from His Crew," Submarine Force Pacific, January 25, 2017, https://www.csp.navy.mil/Media/News-Admin/Article/1059835/submarine-commanding-officer-reflects-on-leadership-lessons-learned-from-his-cr/.

29 "Flashback Friday: When It Absolutely Positively Has To Be There Overnight," Baer Performance Marketing, December 30, 2011, https://baerpm.com/2011/12/30/flashback-friday-when-it-absolutely-positively-has-to-be-there-overnight/.

30 "Frederick W. Smith," Academy of Achievement, last modified June 8, 2022, https://achievement.org/achiever/frederick-w-smith/.

31 Harry Bradford, "FedEx's $5,000 Gamble. Literally." *Huffington Post*, October 15, 2012, https://www.huffpost.com/entry/fred-smith-blackjack-fedex_n_1966837.

32 David Boyle, *Lost at Sea: The Story of the USS Indianapolis* (CreateSpace Independent Publishing Platform, 2016), 120–125.

33 Boyle, *Lost at Sea*, 2.

34 Boyle, *Lost at Sea*, 322–323.

35 "Charles B. McVay III," Wikipedia, last modified June 4, 2023, https://en.wikipedia.org/wiki/Charles_B._McVay_III.

36 Rosemary Giles, "The 50-Year Battle to Clear Charles McVay III In the Sinking of the USS *Indianapolis* (CA-35)," War History Online, March 24, 2023, https://www.warhistoryonline.com/world-war-ii/charles-mcvay-iii-uss-indianapolis.html?edg-c=1&Exc_D_LessThanPoint002_p1=1.

37 Henry Cloud, *Necessary Endings: The Employees, Businesses, and Relationships That All of Us Have to Give Up in Order to Move Forward* (New York: HarperCollins, 2011).

38 Linda T. Kohn, Janet M. Corrigan, and Molla S. Donaldson, *To Err Is Human: Building a Safer Health System* (Washington, DC: National Academy Press, 1999); "Study Suggests Medical Errors Now Third Leading Cause of Death in the U.S.," Johns Hopkins Medicine, News and Publications, May 3, 2016, https://www.hopkinsmedicine.org/news/media/releases/study_suggests _medical_errors_now_third_leading_cause_of_death_in_the_us.

39 Johns Hopkins, "Study Suggests Medical Errors."

40 Robert Campbell, "The Five Rights of Clinical Decision Support: CDS Tools Helpful for Meeting Meaningful Use," *Journal of AHIMA* 84, no. 10 (October 2013): 42–47, https://library.ahima.org/doc?oid=300027.

41 Warren Beardall, "Five Principles about a HRO That You Need to Know," Projects | Within Projects (blog), accessed June 13, 2023, https://projectswithinprojects .blog/2021/10/25/high-reliability-organisation/.

42 David Maxfield et al., "Silence Kills: The Seven Crucial Conversations for Healthcare," VitalSmarts, American Association of Critical-Care Nurses, 2005, https://www.aacn.org/nursing-excellence/healthy-work-environments /~/media/aacn-website/nursing-excellence/healthy-work-environment /silencekills.pdf?la=en.

43 George B. Graen and Mary Uhl-Bien, "Relationship-Based Approach to Leadership: Development of Leader-Member Exchange (LMX) Theory of Leadership Over 25 Years: Applying a Multi-Level Multi-Domain Perspective," *The Leadership Quarterly* 6, no. 2 (1995): 219–247.

44 Graen, "Relationship-Based Approach to Leadership."

45 Arianne Cohen, "How to Quit Your Job in the Great Post-Pandemic Resignation Boom," Bloomberg, May 10, 2021, https://www.bloomberg.com/news /articles/2021-05-10/quit-your-job-how-to-resign-after-covid-pandemic?sref =85rT08Vo#xj4y7vzkg.

46 David Burkus, "Why a Company Is Not a Family – and How Companies Can Bond with Their Employees Instead," ideas.ted.com, January 19, 2022, https://ideas.ted.com/why-a-company-is-not-a-family-and-how-companies -can-bond-with-their-employees-instead/.

47 John Yokoyama and Joseph A. Michelli, *When Fish Fly: Lessons for Creating a Vital and Energized Workplace from the World Famous Pike Place Fish Market* (New York: Hachette Books, 2015).

48 John Cook and Toby Wall, "New Work Attitude Measures of Trust, Organizational Commitment and Personal Need Non-Fulfilment," *Journal of Occupational Psychology* 53 no.1 (March 1980): 39–52, https://doi.org/10 .1111/j.2044-8325.1980.tb00005.x.

49 Don Berwick, *Promising Care: How We Can Rescue Health Care by Improving It* (San Francisco: Jossey-Bass, 2014), 44.

50 Jim Collins, "Good to Great," Jim Collins, Articles, October 2001, https://www.jimcollins.com/article_topics/articles/good-to-great.html.

51 Collins, "Good to Great."

52 Jim Collins, "Level 5 Leadership: The Triumph of Humility and Fierce Resolve," *Harvard Business Review,* January 2001, 64–78, https://hbr.org/2001/01/level-5-leadership-the-triumph-of-humility-and-fierce-resolve-2.

53 Collins, "Level 5 Leadership."

54 Collins, "Level 5 Leadership."

55 Collins, "Level 5 Leadership."

56 Steven D. Levitt, "From Good to Great . . . to Below Average," Freakonomics: The Hidden Side of Everything (blog), July 28, 2008, https://freakonomics.com/2008/07/from-good-to-great-to-below-average/.

57 Theo Winter, "Revisiting a Business Classic: Good to Great (2001)," Human Performance Technology by DTS (blog), February 4, 2019, https://blog.hptbydts.com/revisiting-a-business-classic-good-to-great-2001#; Jim Collins, *How the Mighty Fall and Why Some Companies Never Give In* (Jim Collins, 2009).

58 D. Moore, "'Life Is For Service': The Words That Inspired Mister Rogers," From the Rollins Archives (blog), February 12, 2018, https://blogs.rollins.edu/libraryarchives/2018/02/12/life-is-for-service-the-words-that-inspired-mister-rogers/.

59 Jeff Munroe, "The Mister Rogers Revival," Reformed Journal (blog), December 9, 2019, https://blog.reformedjournal.com/2019/12/09/the-mister-rogers-revival/.

60 Fred Rogers, *Life's Journeys According to Mister Rogers: Things to Remember Along the Way* (New York: Hachette Books, 2013), 85.

61 Charles Colson and Harold Fickett, *The Good Life: Seeking Purpose, Meaning, and Truth in Your Life* (Carol Stream, IL: Tyndale House Publishers, 2006).

62 John 13:13–15 (NIV)

63 "GDP by State," Wisevoter, accessed June 23, 2023, https://wisevoter.com/state-rankings/gdp-by-state/; "Countries by GDP," PopulationU.com, accessed June 23, 2023, https://www.populationu.com/gen/countries-by-gdp.

64 Fred Rogers, "Commencement May 2001," (commencement address, Marquette University, May 2001), https://www.marquette.edu/university-honors/honorary-degrees/rogers-speech.php.